SUPPORTINC
CHILDREN ⌐ı ˉ

This practical guide offers a wealth of advice to support parents and caregivers who have an autistic child within their family.

It provides accessible and straightforward information on the topics that matter most, from initial questions around diagnosis, to providing the best home support. Chapters also debunk myths commonly held about autism and signpost appropriate support mechanisms, including ideas to help with sleep, diet, sensory sensitivities, social interactions, communication, and much more. The emphasis throughout is on offering practical strategies to give much-needed, meaningful support to the child's main caregivers and other family members, in an easily digestible format.

Written from the author's joint perspective as a qualified teacher with an expertise in autism, and as a grandmother of an autistic grandchild, this book is an essential guide for parents and caregivers, created by someone who understands and appreciates what it is like to walk in their shoes.

Dawn Connor currently works as an early years specialist support teacher in Scotland. She is a qualified primary school teacher with over 20 years' experience. Dawn currently advises and works with staff in early years establishments to support young children with additional support needs.

SUPPORTING AUTISTIC CHILDREN AT HOME

A PRACTICAL GUIDE FOR PARENTS
AND CAREGIVERS

Dawn Connor

Routledge
Taylor & Francis Group

LONDON AND NEW YORK

Dedication

I would like to dedicate this book to my family: my mum Jeannette, my husband Joe, my children Barry and Nikki, my two sisters Lesley and Susan and my five grandchildren Chase, Ace, Brodie, Orla, and Matilda.

I would also like to thank my editor, Clare Ashworth, who has been so supportive.

Thank you all for being there for me; it is very much appreciated.

Cover image: Courtesy of Chase Fulton, aged 10

First published 2023
by Routledge
4 Park Square, Milton Park, Abingdon, Oxon OX14 4RN

and by Routledge
605 Third Avenue, New York, NY 10158

Routledge is an imprint of the Taylor & Francis Group, an informa business

British Library Cataloguing-in-Publication Data
A catalogue record for this book is available from the British Library

Library of Congress Cataloging-in-Publication Data
Connor, Dawn, 1964– author.
Title: Supporting autistic children at home : a practical guide for
    parents and caregivers / Dawn Connor.
Description: Abingdon, Oxon ; New York, NY : Routledge, 2023. |
    Includes bibliographical references and index.
Identifiers: LCCN 2022016413 (print) | LCCN 2022016414 (ebook) |
    ISBN 9780367641191 (hardback) | ISBN 9780367641184 (paperback) |
    ISBN 9781003122227 (ebook)
Subjects: LCSH: Parents of autistic children. | Autistic children.
Classification: LCC HQ773.8 .C665 2023 (print) | LCC HQ773.8 (ebook) |
    DDC 649/.154—dc23/eng/20220705
LC record available at https://lccn.loc.gov/2022016413
LC ebook record available at https://lccn.loc.gov/2022016414

ISBN: 978-0-367-64119-1 (hbk)
ISBN: 978-0-367-64118-4 (pbk)
ISBN: 978-1-003-12222-7 (ebk)

DOI: 10.4324/9781003122227

Typeset in Palatino and Scala Sans
by Apex CoVantage, LLC

Contents

Introduction

The fact that you are reading this book might suggest that you may have some questions about how your child, or a child in your family, is developing. Whatever your reason for reading this book, let me reassure you that when you have done so, you should have gained some answers to questions that you may have. More importantly perhaps, you will have been given some practical strategies to help.

There is a wealth of information on the internet about autism, some of it is very good, but some of it is not. This book aims to steer you in the right direction to get current and helpful information about autism.

Each chapter of the book will look at some of the most common aspects when supporting an autistic child, and will detail lots of tried and tested strategies to help with everything from understanding your child's actions, to spending quality time together. It will also give you information about where you can get further advice or support should you require this.

So let me tell you a little bit about me. I am a qualified primary school teacher living in Scotland. I have been teaching for over 20 years, and I have a master's degree in autism (children). But aside from that, I am also a grandmother to five beautiful grandchildren, one of whom is autistic. So I can speak with some understanding of the subject. It is important to say at this point that I do not have an autism diagnosis, but there are many autistic adults who do talk and write about autism through their own lived experiences.

It's also important to say that this book cannot provide a way to diagnose a child as autistic. No book could ever do that, and if one does claim to do so, I would view it with a great deal of scepticism. I can only give you some information about my experiences professionally and personally, and signpost you to further support should you require this.

I hope you enjoy reading this book, and, more importantly, I hope it gives you the answers you seek, or, better, the confidence to support your child in a way that benefits not only them, but *everyone* in your family.

For ease of use throughout the book, I will refer to "autistic children" rather than "children with autism". I have decided to do this after some feedback from autistic adults and through research. Beardon (2019) talks of how autism is not an "add-on" to the person, and, as such, he chooses *not* to use "person *with autism*". When an autistic person is described as *having* autism or is described as a person *with* autism, this is known as "person first" language.

Carpenter, Happe, and Egerton (2019) state that "identity first" language is the preferred choice of many autistic adults, as autism is not something that a person "has".

I will also refer to children who do not have a diagnosis of autism as "non-autistic". Also for ease of use, the pronoun "they" will be used to refer to autistic children. Those with significant responsibility for the care and welfare of autistic children will be referred to as "parents".

CHAPTER 1

Pre-diagnosis – could it be autism?

Perhaps you are reading this book as you may have some questions about how your child is developing and you are looking to find some answers here.

You may have been approached by friends or family members who have suggested that your child might be showing some signs of autism, or you may be wondering yourself if this could be a possibility.

Whatever your incentive for reading, I hope that you will find the answers to any questions you may have.

But first, let me tell you a little bit about my experience. I am a qualified teacher who has taught many autistic children and adults. I have qualifications in autism, and I am well read on the subject. I had no concerns about my grandson, whom some were saying could be autistic. I could not see it. Actually, I did not *want* to see it. And so, for me, he did not "fit the profile". Sure, he was a little slow to speak, his eye contact was not great, he didn't seem to have much in the way of "joint attention" (sharing an interest or time with another person), but I very quickly discounted all those concerns by arguing that many children are slow to speak, but they soon catch up.

Some children are better than others at giving eye contact; perhaps he was one who might just prefer not to look you right in the eye. Perhaps he was just too busy being into his own "thing" and too absorbed in that, to want to share it with anyone else. Besides, he was living in a busy household – lots going on, perhaps he was "lost" in the "hubbub" of everyday life, and he would speak soon. He hadn't yet begun to attend nursery education, so opportunities to experience play with his age and stage peers were limited, perhaps *that* would explain it. His siblings were older, and so I assumed that they were doing the talking for him; that often happens, right? And so on, and so on. He would display really significant sensory sensitivities, and I would try to explain these away by saying "it's just a phase, he'll grow out of it." I was trying to explain away everything with what I thought was a plausible answer.

For his parents, however, the actions that they were witnessing, the lack of speech, and the different sensory reactions displayed by their son really worried them, and led them to their doctor to seek advice. This subsequently led to the involvement of a speech and language therapist, and then, ultimately, to a diagnosis of autism, and this was given when he was 3 years old. I felt numb. To this day, I still find it difficult to accept that I could not, or would not, see it. This is one of the main reasons that I have written this book, in the hope that if *everyone else* has suggested that your child or your grandchild may be autistic, then please put aside your own thoughts, and open up to the possibility that perhaps this is something that is worth exploring. This can be very difficult to do. It is then that you are acknowledging that the hopes and dreams you had planned for your child may take a different path, and it can be upsetting for parents and other family members to come to terms with this. Many parents I have spoken with over the years have talked about feeling a sense of grief – at "losing" the child they had planned for. This is not to say that they were not happy with their child, but, rather, they felt that the plans they had made for them might not come to fruition, and that their child might need much more support than they had imagined they would.

At the time of diagnosis, I felt a sense of dual grief – I was grieving not only for my offspring, but also for my grandson. Now, with lots of hindsight, I can see that this response was wholly wrong, and that my once bleak perspective has changed for the positive, as I see him develop, in his own unique way to become the wonderful individual he is, and I certainly do not grieve the child he might have been had he not been autistic – he is a wonderful child as he is. Many autistic adults are quite rightly upset at the thought that people would be grieving for them as a child. Many autistic adults are also rightly offended by the notion that autism can be viewed by some as a deficit, when, in fact, this is not the case at all. I now feel somewhat guilty that I ever felt so negatively about his diagnosis.

Perhaps, however, you *do* have questions about your child's development, but you need to have your family appreciate that you have these questions. You may suspect it is autism, and you would like to encourage your family member to consider autism as a possibility. You may have already done this and were met with much resistance to the suggestion. Quite often family members can fall out with one another over the raising of such questions about their beloved family member. Perhaps you have seen actions in your child that you feel is not consistent with how you feel they should be developing. Or perhaps you have witnessed actions that you have not seen in your other children as they were growing up. Perhaps it is your first child, and you are perplexed by their actions, which appear different to those of your friends' children, or their peers in nursery.

It may be that you want to have a discussion with your close family members, but you are not quite ready to have "that conversation" with your family. Or perhaps you need to have some "ammunition" before you do have that conversation; to give some "weight" to your thinking. Many grandparents may be, like me, unconvinced, and, more importantly, unwilling, to acknowledge that their grandchild has any kind of disability or difference. Very often they will try to explain it away as merely a child who is not well behaved, or that they require more discipline, routines, or boundaries. This can be problematic when suggestions are made to modify your child's actions, as these can often be at odds with what autistic children actually need. My denial of my grandson's autistic actions led to his parents questioning themselves, and this was not helpful for them – I have since been forgiven.

Whichever scenario best fits your circumstances, there needs to be an understanding of how a non-autistic child presents, and how this would differ in a child who has a diagnosis of autism. Please

3

understand that the comparisons between non-autistic and autistic children throughout this book are there for you to gain an appreciation of the differences. They are not there in any way to make judgements between autistic and non-autistic children. It is very important to make this distinction.

So let's begin by looking at some information about autism.

CHAPTER 2

What is autism?
Myths and facts

So what exactly is autism? While the internet can be a great source of knowledge on a wide variety of subjects, as mentioned earlier, there is a surprising amount of incorrect information about autism. For this reason, please allow me to explain a few myths and a few facts about autism that I have gleaned throughout my years of working with autistic children and through study.

Myth: Everyone is a little bit autistic – we're all somewhere on the autism spectrum.

Fact: Sadly, I hear this very often and it is most certainly not true. While some people may share some of the characteristics of some autistic people such as limited eye contact, this does not mean that they are autistic. Many autistic adults can be quite rightly offended by this statement. You are either autistic, or you are non-autistic, and to say that everyone is a little bit autistic, is to diminish the very real lived experiences of autistic individuals.

Myth: All autistic people experience the world in the same way.

Fact: Not true. If this were true, then the same logic could be applied to all non-autistic individuals, and this is also not true. Some autistic people may experience similar sensory sensitivities, dietary preferences, and communication differences, but this does not make their experiences the same. Some autistic people are preverbal – unable to use words to communicate, while others are very eloquent with speech. Someone once said "when you've met one autistic person, you've met one autistic person" – this is, indeed, so very true.

Myth: Autism is a result of poor parenting.

DOI: 10.4324/9781003122227-2

Fact: This is simply not true. Many people I have worked with have remarked on how they have worried that their child's being autistic was somehow as a result of something they had done, or not done. Many years ago, a man named Bruno Bettelheim came up with the notion that autism was the result of what he called "refrigerator mothers" (Van der Horst, Van Rosmalen, and Van der Veer 2020). He argued, unbelievably, that autism was somehow explained by the lack of interest and/or engagement given by mothers to young autistic infants. For many years this notion had a profoundly negative effect on parents of autistic children. This whole theory has since been totally debunked – and quite rightly too!

Autism is a neurological (brain) developmental condition. This means, in plain speak, that the autistic brain works differently from that of a non-autistic brain. Autism is classed as a disability, although there are many autistic people who do not like the word "disabled" being used to describe them. Many autistic people prefer to use the word "difference", as their view is that "different" does not mean less (Grandin 2020). People who are autistic, experience the world differently from how their non-autistic counterparts experience it.

Myth: Autism is simply naughty behaviour in children.

Fact: Autistic children can display actions that can be different from those of their non-autistic peers, but these are generally connected to their being autistic. These actions usually occur because the child is sensory seeking, has a desire for predictability and routines that are not being met, or because they have difficulties with understanding non-autistic social communication and interactions. Many autistic actions that are seen in children are also as a result of their differences in communicating their needs and wants through speech. I tend to use the word "actions" rather than "behaviour", as "behaviour" implies that the action is deliberate and socially motivated. Very often, this is not the case with autistic children, who are simply *reacting* to events that are out of their control or understanding.

Myth: Autism is an illness that can be cured by treatments.

Fact: Autism is not an illness; neither is it a disease that can be cured with medication or treatments. There are many websites that claim to offer a cure – these should be avoided at all costs. Diseases and illnesses can have cures; autism is neither of these.

Myth: Autistic children can grow out of autism.

Fact: Autism is a lifelong neurodevelopmental condition.

Myth: Autism is a mental health condition that can be helped by counselling.

Fact: Autism is not a mental health condition, but many autistic children and young people can experience anxiety as a result of being autistic (see www.autism.org.uk).

Myth: Anyone with an expertise in autism can give a diagnosis of autism.

Fact: An autism diagnosis is given by medical professionals with an expertise in autism, and if they are not clinicians, they are not in a position to do so. As an experienced teacher with a specialism in autism, I am often asked "do you think my son is autistic?" As I am not a clinician, I would not be able to answer that question.

Myth: Only boys are autistic; autism is a condition seen only in males.

Fact: Not true. Unfortunately, many people still believe this, and think that girls cannot be autistic. This is a common misconception, but it is simply not the case. Although more boys are diagnosed autistic than are girls (see www.autism.org.uk), it is recognised that girls can "mask" or "camouflage" being autistic (Dean, Harwood, and Kasari 2017). Corscadden and Casserly (2021) discuss how parents of autistic girls assigned their daughters' actions to personality "quirks", rather than being connected to being autistic.

In summary: Autism is a different way of seeing and experiencing the world and is concerned with how the brain develops. Autism is not life limiting, neither is it an illness that requires treatment (see www.nhs.uk). It is also not a mental health condition that can be remedied with therapy.

So now we have debunked some common myths about autism, let's have a look now in more detail about what autism can "look like" in reality. Please note that I am not suggesting you use these as a means to diagnose your own, or someone else's, child as autistic. As mentioned earlier, only a clinician can do this. Let's begin with what we might expect to see in autistic babies and children under the age of 5.

PART 1 WHAT YOU MIGHT SEE IN YOUNG AUTISTIC CHILDREN – FROM BABIES TO SCHOOL AGE (USUALLY AGED 5)

[Please remember, no two autistic individuals will present in the same way.]

Social communication and interactions

Social communication and interactions play a huge role in our everyday relationships with family and friends. Enjoying a two-way chat with friends and family, sharing a laugh, and supporting one another through emotional times are all important to us.

For many young autistic children, however, there may be little social motivation or understanding about such social interactions. Temple Grandin (2017) – a world-renowned autistic woman – talks of how, for non-autistic individuals, social understanding is already "innate", in other words, we are born with it, but, for autistic people, this may not be the case. Social communication and interactions are key components of having an autism diagnosis, so this is an important area to discuss. Let's look at this in more detail to analyse what this can "look like" in babies and very young children.

Smith, Segal, and Hutman (2020) suggest that when the following actions are *not* present in young children, this could possibly indicate autism:

- "Back and forth" sharing of smiles, sounds, or "funny faces"
- Pointing, showing, waving "bye bye", or reaching up to be lifted
- Warm and happy expressions shown facially
- Using words
- By the age of 2, using two-word phrases that are not imitated or repeated

Let's look at the first two items on the list: the "back and forth" sharing of smiles, sounds, or "funny faces", and pointing, showing, waving "bye bye", and reaching up to be lifted. All these actions involve something called "joint attention", that is, when two individuals are focussed on the same event or object, and closely monitor one another's attention to that event or object. Studies have shown that there is an atypical response to joint attention in autistic children (Jones and Carr 2004). What this means in plain speak is that if, for example, you use your finger to point to an object and thereby draw your child's attention to that object, they may not follow that "point". Similarly, they may not attempt to gain your attention to objects that *they* find interesting, for example, they may not point to something that they want, or they may not point to show you something that they find interesting. They may also not follow your gaze, for example, if you are looking at something, and then turn your attention suddenly to a different item, they may not follow you in this.

Also mentioned on the list is that babies and very young autistic children might not raise their hands to be lifted. They may also not spontaneously wave "bye bye", even when prompted or encouraged verbally to do so. Similarly, many young non-autistic children will copy an adult's actions such as clapping hands or playing "peek-a-boo". This is something that many autistic children may not do without support from the adult who is playing the game with them.

If we look at the third item on the list, warm and happy facial expressions, many young autistic children can appear to have quite "expressionless" faces, and may find it difficult not only to produce a facial expression, but also to "read" facial expressions of other people (Gordon et al. 2014). It is more common that autistic children will have difficulty in recognising their own emotions, and also the emotions of other people – this is known as "Alexithymia" (Beardon 2019).

When a non-autistic child or adult communicates in response to a smile, gesture, or words that they have received, this is known as "reciprocity". This also happens when we are having a two-way (reciprocal) conversation. In my experience, this is something that some young autistic children may find difficult. It can be especially difficult for parents when this happens, as they may feel that their child is not reflecting back the smiles, cuddles, or affection given by them.

By 12 months of age, a non-autistic young child should be at the "babbling" stage and be seeking to have "back and forth" babbling "conversations" with their parents, and anyone who will listen. Some studies have been undertaken to determine whether a young child's lack or delay in babbling could be an indicator that they may go on to have a diagnosis of autism (Patten et al. 2014). Very young children who are non-autistic will often make a noise in anticipation that someone will copy them, seeking interaction. Very young autistic children may not be socially motivated to make such connections, and may not, therefore, interact in this way.

By around 2 years of age, a non-autistic young child should be following simple verbal requests, gaining an adult's attention to show them things that are of interest to them, pointing to, and naming simple objects and pictures, and generally showing an interest in communicating with others – this is known as "social communication".

At this age (around 2 years), non-autistic children should have a vocabulary of around 50 or more words (see www.autismtoolbox. co.uk/communication), and begin to put two words together, e.g., "bye dada". They will also be copying words and sounds they hear.

Quite often, however, young autistic children are delayed in using speech. This was the case with Temple Grandin, mentioned earlier, who did not speak until she was 3½ years old. She is now a professor of animal science at Colorado State University, an author, and a renowned speaker at conferences around the world.

Many of the young autistic children I have worked with would copy words and sounds they heard. Very often, however, they were using "chunks" of language; what I mean by this, is that they may have heard a few words being used in a phrase and then repeated them. This is known as "echolalia". This simply means that they will echo, or repeat, what they have heard an adult say to them. So for instance, when asked "what would you like for lunch?", they may repeat the question word for word, or simply repeat the last word. Echolalia can be classed as "immediate", as in the lunch question example, or "delayed"; this is where a child will hear a phrase at one point in time, and repeat it later that day or perhaps at an even later stage than that. They may even repeat whole sections of a television show or film.

There are many reasons why echolalia is prevalent in autistic children. Lowry (2016) discusses the ways in which non-autistic and autistic children learn language, and how they differ. Non-autistic children will learn by using single words and gradually build their vocabulary accordingly by putting these together to form sentences and phrases. Autistic children can often follow a different path, by using larger chunks of language that they have heard (with all its grammatical structure), but not yet have an understanding of what each individual word means. For example, they may hear "it's time to have your dinner", and repeat this, but not fully understand what each individual word, in isolation, means. So an autistic child who hears "it's time to have your dinner" may repeat this as a means of *requesting* dinner, as they have formed an association of this learned sentence with this meal.

You might also notice that when echolalia is used in the "dinner" example, an autistic child might use the word "you" when referring to themselves. Reversing pronouns – using "you" instead of "I" in this way, can be common with autistic children. I once worked with an autistic adult who would frequently say "you want" when s*he* wanted to request something.

Some young autistic children, however, display no difficulty in producing speech, but their understanding, or "receptive language", may not be at the same level. So it may be that the child is able to use lots of words and sentences, but they might not understand what is said to them. For example, they may recite a story to you word for word, but if you probe a little more deeply and ask questions about the story, characters, plot, etc., they may find it difficult to answer.

Young autistic children can often speak with an accent that is not spoken by the family. For example, I have worked with many young Scottish autistic children who displayed an American accent, and, in some instances, a "received pronunciation" (RP) accent – similar to that used by English broadcasters in the 1950s. It is more common in autism than in other conditions for speakers in the United Kingdom to speak with an American accent (see www.autismtool box.co.uk/communication).

As young non-autistic children grow and develop, so does their language. At around 3 years of age, they would be expected to have a vocabulary of around 300 words, put four or five words together to make short sentences, and be asking lots of questions (see www. ican.org.uk). It is often at this stage that parents will notice that perhaps their child isn't talking as expected, and that their child may be using other means to communicate their needs; through crying, screaming, or by *looking* at something that they would like, or by taking an adult's hand to something that they want (see www. autism.org.uk). One of the earliest indicators for my grandson's parents was that he was not speaking as expected, and his parents began to wonder if perhaps he were autistic, as he was not communicating using words.

Just before young non-autistic children begin school, they will usually be able to ask and answer "what", "where", and "why" questions, take turns in much longer conversations, understand spoken instructions without stopping their play to look at the speaker, and understand words that describe sequences within events, such as "first", "next", and "later". They can also demonstrate an understanding of what is referred to as "positional language", e.g., using words such as "next to", "behind", "above", and "in between", correctly. These can be difficult concepts for some autistic children at this age.

Very often it is the lack of (or delay in) speech that will alert parents to seek help to understand why their child is finding it difficult to communicate. When this happens, parents are usually referred by their doctor or health visitor to a speech and language therapist. They will then assess the child's language and communication skills, and, if the assessment highlights any areas that require support, they can refer the child for further assessment by a clinician. This was the case with my grandson; his parents were referred to a speech and language therapist who then referred him to a community paediatrician who subsequently gave him an autism diagnosis. It is important to mention that a child will not receive a diagnosis of autism if only one of the diagnostic criteria is present. So if your child is a little slow to speak, but they are meeting their milestones in all other areas, they may not receive a diagnosis.

Social interaction differences can often raise questions for parents. Young non-autistic children by the age of 5 will usually have learned to seek out interactions with their peers, share resources with them, negotiate with them, and have a good awareness of what is socially acceptable, in terms of how to conduct themselves in social settings. Very often, it is within these social areas that parents will notice a difference in how their young autistic children are developing, compared to their non-autistic peers.

Restricted and repetitive patterns of behaviour and interests
Play
Some other indicators of autism at this stage may include how a young child plays. Play for non-autistic children is usually a very sociable occasion. Through play, young children learn key social skills such as sharing and turn taking; very important lessons for future life and relationships. For autistic children, social skills such as these may not be instinctive. Some autistic children may prefer

to spend time with objects, rather than play with a person. I have worked with many parents who talked of how their young child would prefer to sit by the washing machine and watch the clothes spin round and round, rather than play with the toys that had been made available to them.

Another way that play can appear different with autistic children is when they line up their toys in long, neat rows. My grandson used to line up pencils, and I've seen other young autistic children line up Lego™ pieces, rather than click them together to make an object. This type of play is usually done to give some structure or order to events. By doing this, they are giving predictability and purpose to their play, as they may not yet understand *how* to play conventionally. Very often young autistic children have different play skills to those of their non-autistic peers, but they still derive lots of pleasure from how their style of play works out.

Autistic children can often enjoy play that has a repetitive element, for example, emptying and filling containers and stacking cups so that they can knock them over. This would fit with the "restricted, repetitive patterns of behaviours and interests" mentioned in the *DSM-5* (APA 2013) criteria for diagnosing autism. But, as mentioned earlier, many non-autistic children also enjoy this repetitive type of play.

They may also be fascinated by a particular *part* of a toy, e.g., the wheel of a car, spinning it around (rather than playing with the car by moving it up and down a track as a non-autistic child might do).

I have worked a lot with children who will focus on the detail of a particular part of a toy to gain what is called "sensory feedback". This can mean, for example, that in the case of the child examining the wheel of the car, and spinning it around continually, that they may enjoy the visual sensation of its spinning. Similarly, many young autistic children I have worked with have enjoyed the tactile sensation that water play gives them. Some autistic children, however, like it so much, that it can spill over to other areas of the house where there is water, and you can guess what might happen next . . .

You may also see other sensory sensitivities such as the covering of ears when exposed to loud or unexpected noises such as vacuum cleaners, hair dryers, or hand dryers in public toilets.

Toileting
Speaking of toilets, this is an area in which many parents of autistic children under the age of 5 will seek help. I have worked with many young autistic children who were still wearing nappies (diapers) beyond the age of 5. Using the toilet can be a different experience for many young autistic children. When young children attend nursery around age 3, it is commonly accepted that they will already be independent in using the toilet, and will no longer require a nappy. For many young autistic children, however, this is not always the case, and they may not yet be ready to do this independently, and here are some possible reasons why:

- Disliking changes – as mentioned earlier, restricted and repetitive behaviours are part of the diagnostic profile of autism. When an autistic child has been used to wearing a nappy for their whole life so far, it can be very difficult to change this routine (Coucouvanis 2008)
- Difficulty understanding what is expected of them – an autistic child might not understand what it is that you are communicating to them, and, therefore, what they are meant to do (Coucouvanis 2008)
- Sensory differences – some autistic children might not "feel" their body telling them that they need to urinate or defecate (Coucouvanis 2008)
- Diet – some children may have a self-limiting diet, and this may cause constipation (Coucouvanis 2008)

Diet
Speaking of diet, this can be worrying for parents of young autistic children who may be concerned that their child is not getting the right amount of nutrients into their body. Very often, there can be a reluctance to eat what is provided for them, and, often, they may prefer to eat a very plain or "beige" diet. Typically, this would consist of either specific textures of food, such as crunchy items

such as dry cereal, crackers, or toast. Some autistic children might not touch such food, however, preferring to eat smooth foods such as yoghurts or custard. Some autistic children I have worked with have shown preferences for eating only cold food, while others prefer only very hot and spicy food.

Some young autistic children may need close supervision when they eat, as they may overfill their mouths, and eat too quickly.

Eating together is traditionally a very sociable occasion, and this can cause problems for young autistic children who may not yet have an understanding of the social rules around eating. This is often evident when young autistic children are in nursery, and they may take items off another child's plate, or may attempt to retrieve food that has been placed in the bin or that has fallen onto the floor. Similarly, it may be difficult for a young autistic child to appreciate why they should remain seated at the table until others have finished, or to wash their hands before eating. They may also not display an understanding of the routines involved with having snack. It is important to say here that these actions are not deliberate on the part of the autistic child, but, rather, are borne out of being autistic, and not having an awareness of the *social* rules around eating.

Many young autistic children can gag at the mere smell or visible presence of food that they do not want to eat. Also, if food items on the plate are touching one another, this can also be a "deal breaker" for autistic children, and they will often not want to eat anything on the plate. Please bear in mind that this is not just "picky" eating, but a real sensory aversion to food that they do not want near them. This leads me onto the next topic, that of the senses.

Sensory sensitivities
I know we all talk about having five senses, right? But, no, there are actually eight, and they are:

- Visual (sight)
- Auditory (hearing)

- Tactile (touch)
- Olfactory (smell)
- Gustatory (taste)
- Proprioceptive (body position and self movement)
- Vestibular (balance)
- Interoceptive (internal state of the body)

Sensory sensitivities are also mentioned within the *DSM-5*, as many autistic children display sensory differences (see www.autism.org. uk). These can have a profound effect on how an autistic child experiences the world, and this, in turn, can have a significant effect on how they react to everyday sounds, smells, and touch that non-autistic people take for granted, such as taking a trip to the supermarket.

Typically, senses can be categorised as being under-sensitive – also known as "hyposensitive", or oversensitive – also known as "hypersensitive". So, for example, the child who is covering their ears when the hand dryer is on could be described as having auditory hypersensitivity (*avoiding* more *auditory* feedback). Similarly, the child who is continually spinning objects could be described as having visual hyposensitivity (*seeking* more *visual* feedback).

Let's examine the first sense on our list: visual. When a child is hyposensitive to light, items can appear darker than they are. Depth perception can be poor, resulting in a child who finds it difficult to throw and catch a ball, and who is prone to tripping up when walking. They may also find that their peripheral vision is blurred, but objects in the centre of their vision may be magnified. When they are hypersensitive visually, images that they see may be fragmented, bright lights and objects may appear to move around, and they may be very sensitive to light, covering their eyes (see www.autism.org.uk).

Next on the list is the auditory (hearing) sense. Many young autistic children can display hypersensitivity with this sense, and, as mentioned earlier, will cover their ears if sounds are too loud. This typically happens when they are in busy shops, shopping malls, public toilets with loud hand dryers, or, as discussed previously, when someone is vacuuming or using a hairdryer. This hypersensitivity to sound is something I have witnessed when young children first come into a nursery setting where there is typically a lot of noise from the other children. You may also witness this in autistic children when sudden and unexpected noises happen, such as fire alarms, car horns, thunder, dogs barking, and during firework displays.

Reactions to sudden and unexpected loud noises can appear quite extreme in autistic children. I have witnessed children who will scream, attempt to run off, hit out at others who are nearby, engage in what is called "stimming" or self-stimulating actions such as rocking back and forth, flapping hands, "flicking" their fingers, jumping, tapping objects, and many other actions that serve to soothe and calm autistic children. They may also attempt to injure themselves by biting their hands or banging their head on the floor – referred to as "self-injurious" actions.

Next on the list is that of the tactile sense. If a young autistic child is hypersensitive to this sense, they can often react in ways that a non-autistic child may not. For example, they may scream if someone brushes past them and briefly touches them, or they may not like the feeling of clothing labels rubbing on their back – this can often result in a young child stripping off, and this can be very upsetting for all concerned. Similarly, they may want to walk about without their socks and shoes on. Babies, likewise, may find nappy changing distressing.

If a young autistic child is hyposensitive to the tactile sense, then you may see that they don't appear upset if they fall over. They may seem to have hurt themselves, they may even be bleeding, but the child doesn't react by crying or even appear to show that they are in pain.

Now the next sense can explain perhaps why some young autistic children have a self-limiting diet, preferring specific items. The olfactory sense is simply our sense of smell. Hypersensitivity to this sense can result in a child displaying a real aversion to smells by gagging, vomiting, or displaying actions such as those mentioned earlier, e.g., hitting out. New smells such as changes to perfume, laundry detergent, soap, or toothpaste might bring about such reactions to someone who has a sensory aversion to new, unfamiliar, or unpleasant smells.

Hyposensitivity to this sense can be seen in young autistic children who will actively sniff out people – up close and personal. They may also attempt to sniff, and explore, the contents of their nappy.

The next sense is the one concerned with eating – the gustatory sense. Hypersensitivity to this sense can be seen in a young autistic child who finds teeth cleaning really uncomfortable. They may also only eat items that are smooth, such as yoghurts. This type of hypersensitivity may explain why some children can find it difficult to visit the dentist.

Hyposensitivity to this sense can result in a young autistic child who will "mouth" everything. They may also display what is called "Pica" – this is when a child will attempt to eat inedible items, for example, grass, dirt, or sand. They may also grind their teeth, and attempt to bite others for no obvious (to those who are watching) reason.

The last three on the senses list may be unfamiliar to you, so let's discuss these in more detail.

Proprioception tells us where we are in relation to our environment. For example, if I close my eyes and touch my nose with my finger, I am using my proprioceptive sense. Similarly, if I walk on the pavement and look straight ahead without having to look at my feet, I am also demonstrating a good use of proprioception. This is the subconscious sense that allows us to figure out what our limbs are doing without looking at them.

The vestibular sense is located in the inner ear, and is connected with our balance. For example, it stops us falling if we bend over. Hypersensitivity with the vestibular sense can result in a dislike of, for example, moving walkways, going on escalators, or using swings. Hyposensitivity of this sense can be seen in young autistic children who seek out these particular movements and actions.

Finally, the interoception sense is one that tells us if we are hungry, thirsty, hot, or cold. It also lets us know that our bladder or bowels need emptying. I have worked with many young autistic children who attempt to throw off their jacket and run out into the snow, apparently not feeling the cold. Similarly, I have worked with young autistic children who will insist on wearing many layers of clothing on a warm summer's day – seemingly unaware that they are turning bright red in the face with the warmth of the extra clothing.

All the senses mentioned are experienced by autistic and non-autistic children on a daily basis, and when participating in everyday routines. Let's look now at how some of these can impact on young autistic children, beginning with some events that may be more challenging for them.

Going on visits to the supermarket/dentist/
doctor/hairdresser
These are areas in which many young autistic children find it difficult to cope, and you may, as a result of this, see the following actions:

- Refusal to leave the house
- Throwing themselves to the floor
- Screaming or hitting out
- "Stimming" actions such as rocking, flapping their hands, making loud noises
- Self-injurious actions such as banging their head on the floor or with their hand(s), punching their leg, biting their hand

This can be very upsetting to anyone watching, as there may be no obvious reason why a shopping trip, for example, could be difficult, but given the sensory sensitivities, the resistance to change, not being able to predict what is going to happen, and the difficulties with social communication and interactions, it begins to make more sense, doesn't it?

The same actions can often be seen when a young autistic child is taken to the doctor, dentist, or for a hospital check-up. Very often these places are quite clinical with very bright lights, noisy machines, and lots of people. The clinician may use tools to examine them, and they may be unaware of the autistic child's differences with sensory sensitivities, social communication, and interactions. As a result, a typical examination may turn out to be very stressful for an autistic child who has no awareness of why they are there in the first place, let alone any understanding of why this person is, for example, putting a cold, hard tool into their mouth to check their teeth. Perhaps they can't use speech to indicate that this is not comfortable for them, and so they may resort to protesting in other ways that might seem inappropriate to the onlooker.

Sleeping
Many parents I have worked with have had concerns about their child's sleeping patterns. Sleep can often be a very big issue for the parents of autistic children, as some find it difficult to get to sleep. Many autistic children can often be awake until the early hours of the morning, and this can cause much disruption to family life as a consequence of parents themselves losing sleep. It is not uncommon for very young autistic children to come into nursery very tired, and, occasionally, to fall asleep later on in the session. Sleep can be different for autistic children for a few reasons, including the following (see www.autism.org.uk):

- Not understanding that others in the house going to bed means that *they* need to sleep
- Difficulty with winding down, to settle to sleep
- Being distracted by what is referred to as "blue light" emitted from screens such as the television or other electronic devices
- Irregularity of melatonin – this is the sleep hormone that regulates the pattern of sleep

So, as you can see, life can be very difficult for young autistic children and their families. We'll now look at what can happen when they move into the next phase of their life – going to school.

PART 2 WHAT YOU MIGHT SEE IN YOUNG AUTISTIC CHILDREN AT PRIMARY (ELEMENTARY) SCHOOL AGE

[Please remember, as always, no two autistic individuals will present in the same way.]

Many of the areas that were discussed in Part 1 will still be present at this stage – and possibly may remain throughout life. Sensory sensitivities related to diet, clothing, and loud noises can still be challenging for many autistic children at school. Some may still not be fully independent in using the toilet, and may require assistance with this. Some autistic children may not yet be speaking, and so it is very important to say that a young autistic child's first formal school experience may be different from that of their non-autistic peers.

It may be that they attend a school that is more suited to their specific educational requirements. This could be a specialist classroom contained within a mainstream school, or it could be a standalone specialist school for children who have additional support needs. How this is achieved may be different where you live, but if you have concerns about how your child may cope with moving into the next phase of their educational journey, then it's advisable to speak with their nursery teacher or other educational professional in advance to voice your concerns, if this has not already been done by them.

It is also very important to say that many autistic children will attend their local primary (elementary) school with their peers. It is not uncommon for children to receive their autism diagnosis when they are already in school. Perhaps they have coped well until starting school, but differences in key areas such as social communication and interactions, sensory sensitivities, and dietary differences can become more apparent.

Social communication and interaction differences can also mean that once they have started school, autistic children may not wish to discuss how their day has been with their parents. Some autistic children can also find school so overwhelming in terms of sensory sensitivities and social communication and interaction differences, that they may become very distressed at the mention of going to school, and some may refuse to go altogether.

Very often, autistic children can "keep it together" until they get home from school, and this is often when it can become too much for them, and they have to find a "release". This can often result in what is commonly called a "meltdown" or "shutdown". This can happen as an extreme response to being overwhelmed. This is not ever to be confused with a temper tantrum. Some actions you may witness in a "meltdown" could include refusing to interact with you, withdrawing to a safe place, shouting, screaming, being upset, stripping off their clothes, being physical (kicking, hitting), self-injurious actions such as biting their hand, slapping themselves, or punching themselves. This can be very frightening for parents to witness, but it is not uncommon, and more will be discussed later in the book about how you can help, if this is something that you encounter with your child.

Would now be a good time to mention homework? I ask this as it is an issue for many autistic children who find it difficult to understand that school work is for school, and not for home, and so when parents present them with homework, this can also lead to a "meltdown".

As mentioned earlier, restricted and repetitive patterns of behaviour and interests are key components of an autism diagnosis. This can present itself in many ways at school. Having predictability to their school day is extremely important for autistic children, and so when changes to their routines happen, it can be very distressing. Changes that can naturally occur in school could include having their teacher absent due to sickness or training, with a new teacher replacing them, very often at short notice. Another change could be that they have a special event such as a fundraiser day where they have to dress up in different clothing, or if they are celebrating festivals such as Hallowe'en where costumes are expected to be worn. Sensory sensitivities to loud music, different fabrics on the skin, party food, and so on, can all present as challenges to autistic children, and they may not have the communicative skills, or feel the need to, express their displeasure, so it is understandable that they may then use other means of expressing this such as "shutting down".

On the flip side, many young autistic children relish the opportunity that the structure and predictability of school brings to them. Schools are places where rules are in place, and many autistic children enjoy, and can be very good at, following rules. Quite often they may take on the role of "rule keeper", and may try to correct others in their class (and the teacher) if rules are not followed explicitly. This can sometimes lead to autistic children being ostracised from their peers, or, worse, excluded from school altogether.

Having friendships with peers can also be a challenge for some autistic children, and they may prefer to spend a lot of their free time on their own. This can be difficult for family members to understand, and they may try to "push" them into becoming more sociable. This can lead to much upset on the part of the child, and can be counterproductive. This can often occur when they are invited to a school friend's birthday party – this may sound like good fun to the parent, but perhaps this could be sensory overload for the autistic child who understandably may not want to go.

Autistic children can often excel in subjects such as mathematics, computing, languages, and art, but might struggle with physical education activities or with the fine motor skills required for handwriting. Some autistic children can be their own worst critics, and a fear of "failing" in some way at school can cause them great distress. I have previously witnessed children in my class who have become so concerned about the "accuracy" of their letter formation and handwriting, that they have gone into a "meltdown" simply because they have made one simple mistake. Sometimes, this heightened attention to detail can lead to the child not wishing to go to school, as they feel that they may make further "errors".

As discussed earlier, autistic children tend to cope better in school when there is predictability to their day. Having the same teacher each day, the same seat on which to sit, the same peers in their classroom are all helpful in giving this reassurance that changes are kept to a minimum. Problems can arise when autistic children transition into high school, so let's look at how this can affect them.

PART 3 WHAT YOU MIGHT SEE IN AUTISTIC TEENAGERS

[Please remember, as always, no two autistic individuals will present in the same way.]

Going from one class in a local primary school to a larger high school can be challenging for autistic children for a number of reasons. Let's examine these in more detail.

First, high school buildings are larger in size, and, as a result, have many more people. This can be significantly overwhelming in terms of the sensory elements: too many people can mean too much noise and many more smells. This is especially true at lunchtime and at break times when students tend to be louder as they chat to their peers, and also with all of the smells in the lunch hall. When students move around the corridors of their high school, they will often bump into or brush past one another, and this can be sensory overload for someone who has hypersensitivity to touch.

Second, there is more than one classroom to attend: different environments for different subjects can be confusing, and all of the movements between each classroom can be challenging to the senses. There are many more teachers' names to remember, and there will be different students in different classes – which can also be confusing. Having so many teachers can also mean that there are many more opportunities for changes to happen, e.g., more possibility of supply (substitute) teachers being brought in for absences.

Third, examinations: these can cause undue stress and put pressure on the autistic student who may be a perfectionist and find failure extremely difficult to accept.

Fourth, homework: especially as there will be a lot more of it, given that they have more subjects to learn. This can cause problems when they come home and want to have "time out" to gain the "release" mentioned earlier, but have to do homework instead.

Fifth, hormones: puberty can be a very challenging time for autistic adolescents: their bodies are changing, their emotions are heightened, they are often more easily tired, and girls begin menstruating – this can be very alarming to young autistic girls.

It is therefore perfectly understandable that autistic adolescents might not enjoy high school as much as their non-autistic counterparts.

So what can be done to help? Chapter 4 details some useful strategies that can be used to support autistic children from birth through to adulthood. But before we skip too far into the future, the next chapter will examine some common thoughts and feelings should your child or grandchild receive a diagnosis of autism.

CHAPTER 3
Post-diagnosis

So the assessment has happened and your child has been given a diagnosis of autism, and you are probably wondering "what happens next?".

My grandson's parents were given the news and were then asked if they had any questions. They were then handed a couple of leaflets highlighting local organisations that could offer advice and support, and the appointment was over. Many of the parents I have spoken with over the years have described similar experiences when their child's diagnosis had been given. Many were handed leaflets but were too bewildered by the news to think of asking questions, and many were upset. Some even described how they left the consultation feeling "lost", and, often, thinking of the many questions they could have asked after the consultation had ended.

Quite often, as mentioned earlier, the first port of call for information about this newly diagnosed condition is the internet. As discussed before, this is not always a good idea, as there is a lot of misleading information on the internet about autism. If you do feel the need to do some research on autism, then there are some trusted sites mentioned in Chapter 5 that will give good, safe advice, but I hope this book will give you all of the information you seek.

It's not uncommon for parents to feel a whole variety of emotions when their child is diagnosed as autistic. For my grandson's parents, their overwhelming feeling was one of relief: that what they had been witnessing in terms of my grandson's actions, the sensory reactions, and the communication differences were there for a reason that made sense to them – he was autistic. They also felt a little sad and worried. They were anxious about how he would fare in school, and, beyond this, into adulthood. I remember speaking to a parent who told me about their fears for when their child would be

DOI: 10.4324/9781003122227-3

an adult and what that would bring – their child was only 3 years old at the time. This is not uncommon. It's a parent's instinct to want the best for their child, and when you receive news that your child has any form of disability or difference, you naturally want to project into the future to imagine what life could be like for them, and, in so doing, predict what harm may lie in their path, so that you can protect them. Trust me when I say that you should take each day as it comes, and try not to imagine your child's whole life ahead of them – no one can predict the future for any child.

One of the most common feelings that I have witnessed parents experience is that of denial. Like me, some do not want to acknowledge that there is anything different about their child. It can often be difficult to accept a diagnosis, and this can sometimes lead to arguments between partners and other family members. Quite often grandparents (and parents) will not even have heard of autism, and will immediately type the word "autism" into an internet search engine. Another reason that this can be unhelpful is that quite often they may find videos of autistic children whose actions and speech do not match those of their own grandchild, and they could then assume that there must have been a mistake with the diagnosis. As autistic individuals are just that – individuals – there can be confusion as to why a doctor has said that their grandchild has the same condition as the child whom they had seen on their computer.

Many grandparents, like me, do not want to acknowledge that their precious grandchild might need support, and they may feel overwhelmed, as I did, about what lay ahead for them, and for their parents. When grandparents are in denial of the condition, however, it isn't helpful for anyone, and I'm speaking from first-hand experience here.

Other feelings can bubble to the surface when a diagnosis is given, and that can include blame. Parents can often blame one another for the diagnosis, and, sometimes, grandparents can blame the parents – "if only you had disciplined him better", or "he must get that from you." Again, this is not helpful for anyone. Lack of discipline does not cause autism – let's make that very clear. How a parent interacts with their child does not cause autism – let's also make that very clear. To put it simply, a child is *born* autistic, and there is no reason to place blame. To use the word "blame" is to say that something is wrong for there to be a problem to "blame". Your child (their grandchild) is not a problem, but, rather, a person whom you all love, so why should blame even be mentioned?

There are many parents who might feel quite angry about the diagnosis. They may think that the doctor has made a mistake, and that their child is just going through a phase, and that when they are older, things will change and everything will be fine. They may also feel "why my child?" – and this is not an uncommon response. At the end of the day, your child is still your child – autism diagnosis or not, and the love you have for them does not diminish with this diagnosis.

For my grandson's parents, there were a lot of emotions including worry. They were worried about how he would cope with school – would he be vulnerable? Would he be bullied because of his vulnerability? Their fears, and how his differences were presenting, led them to seek a specialist educational provision for him – a school where children with additional support needs are taught. They were very lucky to be offered a place, and he is thriving so well in this type of environment. Grandparents, however, may be a little unsure about the idea of a different school for their grandchild. This could stem from their own perceptions of what this could look like, based, perhaps, on schools they had heard of, or known, when *they* were growing up. Very often the mention of a different school can lead to arguments with grandparents because of this. Nowadays, there are specialist classes within mainstream schools, and perhaps these weren't available when some grandparents were at school themselves.

Through my experience as both a teacher and a grandmother, I have gained a good understanding of the importance of meeting the needs of children in school. Whatever form the school takes, if it is meeting the needs of the child emotionally and educationally, then that is what is most important. For me, it doesn't matter that my grandson is learning in a school for children who have additional support needs. What matters is that he is learning at a pace and in an environment that is best suited to his particular circumstances and requirements.

Some parents may feel a little sad that their autistic child will not be going to the same school as their non-autistic sibling, but the needs of their autistic child might be such that their sibling's school just may not suitable for them in terms of the curriculum or the environment.

Speaking of siblings, a diagnosis can be difficult idea for them to accept, too. They may feel that their sibling is getting all of this extra attention spent on them, and they may understandably feel a little left out. For some, however, they may feel a closer bond to them, and want to protect them. Some may feel uncomfortable when out and about with their autistic sibling, especially if they have sensory differences. There could be embarrassment if their autistic sibling reacts to something in a way that is different to how "unknowing eyes" from a stranger would expect them to react, e.g., sensory overload in a supermarket. As an autistic child does not have a visually obvious disability, reactions from the public can sometimes be quite cruel, and this may cause siblings to feel anxious.

All these emotions are easy to understand when faced with a lifelong condition that has no cure. It is important to say that how you and your family reacts to the diagnosis is entirely an individual reaction, and that there is no right way to react.

There are many, many autistic people who are rightly unhappy about the perception that an autism diagnosis is viewed in negative terms. Many of these autistic people would not want their diagnosis changed if given the opportunity to do so, and it is important to recognise and respect their viewpoints on this. How you and your family view the diagnosis is key to how your child is supported; a positive outlook can certainly help to achieve a positive outcome. What is also important is how you and your family can help to support one another to meet your child's needs. There are many ways that you can do this, and these will be discussed next.

CHAPTER 4

Practical strategies

Within this chapter, you will find some helpful suggestions and strategies to support your child according to the categories mentioned in Chapter 2. The strategies are suitable for any family member to use. It would actually be very helpful if all family members could adopt the same strategies, as this would give a consistency of approach and predictability to your child. If everyone were to adopt different ones, this could possibly lead to confusion, which could lead to potentially upsetting your child.

I thought it would be helpful if the strategies were written in age order, but it is very important to highlight at this point that your child's *chronological* age (how old they are), might not be the same as their *developmental* age (how they are presenting). For example, grandparents might expect that their autistic grandchild should be doing things at their chronological age, such as using the toilet independently by the age of 3. As mentioned in Chapter 2, using the toilet independently may happen later for autistic children than non-autistic peers, (but also may not), so it's not helpful to put a particular age on this.

Your child may also be at a stage where they are "crossing into" a different age group, so please consider your child's particular circumstances when viewing these strategies – perhaps some strategies detailed in Part 2 (children aged 5–12) may be more suited to your child at a younger or older age – it all depends on your child's individual situation.

The strategies in this section can support the following areas of difference:

- Social communication and interaction
- Sensory sensitivities (including dietary differences and sleep)

DOI: 10.4324/9781003122227-4

- Going on visits
- Attending medical appointments

As you can see, "behaviours" have not been included anywhere in this book. As mentioned earlier, any *actions* that your child might display will more often than not be as a result of differences experienced by your child in any one of these categories. Hopefully, most of the areas where you may see differences in your child's responses, compared to their non-autistic peers, might be supported by implementing these strategies.

Each of the categories is listed as follows:

- *What* action you might see
- *Possible reasons why* you might see it
- *How you might be able to help*

Some of these suggested strategies may not suitable for your child's particular needs/preferences, therefore please view these as *possibilities* rather than *"must dos"*.

So let's begin working our way through the list, looking at each of the areas in order, and examine how these can be presented in young autistic children, beginning with Part 1 – children under the age of 5.

PART 1 CHILDREN UNDER THE AGE OF 5

Social communication and interaction

What	Possible reasons why
Continually crying (at bedtime) It's important to note that not all autistic babies will cry at bedtime, some will be very quiet – just like non-autistic children, no two autistic children are the same	1 Feeling too hot or cold 2 Material scratching against skin 3 Lighting too bright 4 Too much visual stimulation 5 Too little visual stimulation 6 Too much noise 7 If crying occurs after bottle feeding, possible milk intolerance 8 Teething
How you might be able to help	
1 Remove or add layers as appropriate – trial and error to see if this helps 2 Remove labels from clothing and bedding. Wash everything with fabric softener (be mindful of the scent of the fabric softener, as it may be overpowering for your child) 3 Use a dimmer switch or light that gradually gets dimmer as the night passes. Use blackout blinds to block outside light 4 Lessen the amount of wall displays in the bedroom (pictures, highly patterned wallpaper etc.) 5 Place a cot "mobile" over the cot for visual stimulation 6 Remove or quieten televisions from nearby rooms. Remove any ticking clocks. Close windows. Where possible, provide them with their own bedroom – this will help to minimise distraction, and encourage better sleep 7 Speak with your health visitor or doctor to check whether your child might have a milk intolerance 8 Follow advice from your health visitor or doctor	

Figure 4.1

Social communication and interaction

What	Possible reasons why
Not using words to communicate	Many young children who are autistic may be late to speak, some may never speak, while others may speak from an early age

How you might be able to help

- Consult with a speech and language therapist (pathologist) – this should ideally be your first port of call. They may recommend different ways that your child can be taught to communicate such as Makaton™. This is a method of communication that some preverbal children can use to communicate by means of *signing*. They may also recommend PECS – Picture Exchange Communication System (https://pecs-unitedkingdom.com) as a means of communicating their needs and wishes, using *pictures*

- Give them a reason to want to communicate – use their interests to encourage this

- Try to be at your child's level when speaking with them

- Be mindful that some children cannot look at you and listen to you at the same time, so *please don't insist on eye contact*

- Speak more slowly than you would when you are speaking to a non-autistic child. This is to help your child should they require time to process what you are saying to them. In my experience, some young autistic children can take 20 seconds to process

- Keep your words short and to the point, for example "Johnny, bedtime" rather than "Johnny, it's time to go to bed now, you look tired, and you need your sleep." Using too many words can be confusing

- Label items *verbally*, e.g. saying "spaghetti", "television" etc., when your child is presented with them. Speaking these words every day will enable them to make the connection between the object and the spoken word. In time, this might encourage them to say the word should they want to request the item

- Don't ask them to copy what you are saying; this isn't helpful and might confuse them even more

Figure 4.2

Social communication and interaction

What	Possible reasons why
Making sounds (known as "vocalisations")	Some autistic children may begin "babbling" at a later stage than their non-autistic peers
How you might be able to help	

- Acknowledge these sounds, and, where possible, extend them by adding different sounds. Communication is about making a connection with another person, so it's good to try to encourage any sounds your child makes when they are attempting to communicate
- If the sound your child is making sounds like a word, model how the word *should* be said, if they were able to say it

Figure 4.3

Social communication and interaction

What	Possible reasons why
Making loud vocalisations – screaming/shouting	**Pain**
	1 Just as some young autistic children can find it difficult to communicate their needs and wants, they can also struggle to communicate if they are in pain
	Sensory sensitivities
	2 Loud vocalisations can often occur during nappy changes due to sensory sensitivities
	Changes to routines
	3 These can be difficult for autistic children to understand due to **restricted, repetitive patterns of behaviour and interests** (*APA 2013*)
How you might be able to help	

1 As you would with a non-autistic child, seek medical advice if you are concerned that they may be in pain, but cannot communicate this to you verbally

2 Try placing a soft, fluffy towel on the changing mat – a cold hard surface could cause sensory overload

3 Look for patterns: does this occur at set times/in set places/ usually when "x" happens. It's always a good idea to observe when and where it occurs, to identify a possible connection with a time, place, event, person, smell, sound, texture, food. Try to eliminate one item at a time to see if this helps. If it occurs at a time when you change a set routine suddenly, e.g., going a different way to the shops, or going on an unexpected visit to the doctor's, then please see section on "visits" for advice on how best to approach this

Figure 4.4

Social communication and interaction

What	Possible reasons why
Repeating words or phrases – known as "echolalia"	To acknowledge understanding by repeating instructions back to the person giving them
	To achieve a sense of calm
	For reassurance – talking aloud the steps of a sequence can help to give this
	To rehearse what they may say later (Prizant with Fields-Meyer 2015)
	To communicate choices

How you might be able to help

- Acknowledge their attempt to communicate, and please do not ask them to stop

- Try to establish where and when they are using echolalia to communicate their needs or wants. For example, if they are repeating "time for snack" (from a familiar phrase used in their nursery), then perhaps they are trying to communicate to you that they are hungry or thirsty

- Respond as if you were speaking for them, e.g., if they were to say "time for snack", then it would be good for you to acknowledge and respond to this request with "you want snack?" Note that I have not used any social "niceties" here, "please" and "thank you" can be taught later – better to focus on the communication element first

Figure 4.5

Social communication and interaction

What	Possible reasons why
Repeating words or phrases – perhaps from a favourite television show or film out of context (i.e., not in the moment)	Delayed echolalia Self-soothing if stressed (coping mechanism) Like echolalia, but repeating words in this way may occur days/weeks after the event
How you might be able to help	
• Again, acknowledge this, as before with echolalia. Perhaps this might be the way that a request to watch that film or television show is being communicated?	

Figure 4.6

Social communication and interaction

What	Possible reasons why
Taking toys, food, or other items from siblings	This is a tricky one for family members to appreciate. At a surface level, it could be viewed as your child being mean or deliberately naughty. For an autistic child, the reason might simply be that they don't yet have an understanding that this is not what is expected of them – difficulty with understanding social "rules". It could also be that they just don't have the words yet to communicate their wishes to their sibling, and so simply taking items could be their means of communicating that they want the item

How you might be able to help

- Demonstrate to your child how to ask for these things using simple language or gestures, e.g., holding out their hand or saying one word to request (if this is possible), e.g., "please?"

- Perhaps have two of each toy – reinforcing which toy belongs to which child

- If food is being grabbed from plates, try seating children at opposite ends of the table

- You could also try to model to them how to ask for more food by having ready an extra amount that they could request from you

- It might be that they look at the plate to indicate that they would like some more – this could be their way of communicating "more". If this happens, I would model the word "more?" to them and wait for them to respond in some way, either by reaching out for the object or looking at you or the object. As mentioned earlier, don't insist on eye contact, but if they do manage to make eye contact, then take this as a non-verbal gesture to indicate "yes" and respond immediately

Figure 4.7

Sensory sensitivities – auditory (hearing) hypersensitivity – (avoiding)

What	Possible reasons why
Hands over ears – this may be accompanied by loud vocalisations	This is very common in young autistic children, and in many older children and adults too. This can be very frightening for children, as their hearing can be so acute, that sounds can hurt their ears. Sometimes it can be the suddenness of the noise, not knowing where the sound is coming from, or the lack of being able to control it, that can upset autistic children

How you might be able to help

Make a note of when this occurs – it may occur when the hairdryer or vacuum cleaner is on, the television or radio is too loud, the doorbell rings, a dog barks, the telephone rings, a voice is raised loudly, someone sneezes, a balloon bursts, or being in crowded places, to name but a few. Here are some ways to help:

- Have the hairdryer, vacuum cleaner, telephone, and any other electronic devices on at the quietest setting. Give advanced warning that you're going to switch it on. Practise switching it on and off. Invite your child to do this too (safety being paramount). Make a game of it by practising using the equipment with your child, e.g., drying dolly's hair, vacuuming the carpet. Try to gradually desensitise them to it very gently. If they become visibly upset, then discontinue

- If the noisy doorbell is too loud, could you put a sign next to it saying "please ring once only"? As with the hairdryer, have your child press the bell and make a game of it (if they can cope with this)

Figure 4.8

- Blow up a balloon and release it gently to allow small bits of air to be released (making a sound). Perhaps they can pop the balloon (to have the control over when the noise happens)
- Turn down the ringtone on telephones and devices
- Avoid noisy environments where possible – e.g., shop at quieter times or online
- Provide ear defenders or headphones with music to see if this will help – although it is important to note that some autistic children might not like to have these on their head due to sensory sensitivities to touch
- Lower your voice volume when speaking

Figure 4.8 (Continued)

Sensory sensitivities – auditory hyposensitivity – (seeking)

What	Possible reasons why
Displays no reaction to loud or sudden sounds	1 Engrossed in their own activity – autistic children are often referred to as "being in their own world". When this happens, they can often "zone" out of what is happening around them, so that they can focus on what they enjoy doing
Doesn't respond when spoken to by others	2 This is often mistaken as the child's being rude by not responding, but it can also be for the reason mentioned above
Making repetitive noises	3 Seeking auditory feedback

How you might be able to help

1 Initially, it is a good idea to have your child's hearing checked by an audiologist to rule out any issues with hearing

2 Try to be as animated as possible to gain their attention – this might involve singing to them, or lightly tapping them on the arm when saying their name. Come down to their level so that they can hear and see you more clearly. Again, please don't insist on eye contact, they may well be listening, but just not *looking*. Try approaching them from the front to avoid any sudden or unexpected surprise. Always say their name before giving instructions or engaging verbally with them – in this way, they will know that you are talking with *them*, and not with someone else in the room

3 Limit the time spent on toys and activities with repetitive sounds as this could cause overstimulation. It's a good idea to show the time allowed on the activity visually – e.g., using a timer on your phone that counts down, or an egg or sand timer to show how long is left to do this activity. Once it is finished, remove it from their vision discretely – if it remains in view of the child, they may still think it is available to them. Redirect to an alternative activity that the child enjoys such as a "people game" or playing "catch the bubbles" using a bubble machine or wand

Figure 4.9

Sensory sensitivities – visual hypersensitivity – (avoiding)

What	Possible reasons why
Covering eyes – possibly crying while doing this	1 Lighting too bright
	2 Too much visual stimulation

How you might be able to help

1

- Use blackout blinds
- Have dimmer switches fitted to lighting
- Avoid fluorescent lighting as this can not only be harsh to view, but can emit a buzzing sound that can upset some autistic children
- Allow sunglasses or hats to be worn in brightly lit areas
- Avoid seating next to windows where light can suddenly and unexpectedly change

2

- Check vision with an ophthalmologist (eye doctor)
- Avoid visually "busy" environments, for example, try not to have highly patterned wallpaper, curtains, or carpets in bedrooms

Figure 4.10

Sensory sensitivities – visual hyposensitivity – (seeking)

What	Possible reasons why
Holding objects very closely to their eyes	1 Short-sighted vision
	2 Seeking visual stimulation
	3 To focus on the object itself, and thereby screen out the surrounding objects

How you might be able to help

1 Check vision with a qualified optician. More about how best to facilitate medical appointments will be discussed later in the book

2 As with the auditory seeking of repetitive noises, limit the amount of time spent on light-up toys as these can overstimulate. I need to emphasise here that "stimming" or sensory seeking stimulation, *should not be discouraged*, as this can help to soothe an autistic person when they are distressed or anxious

3 It may be the case that the *peripheral* vision is being used more than looking straight at objects through the central vision. Try moving into their peripheral vision "zone" to engage with them

Figure 4.11

Sensory sensitivities – tactile hypersensitivity – (avoiding touch)

What	Possible reasons why
Dislikes cuddles	Tactile hypersensitivity

How you might be able to help

Seek advice and guidance from a therapist who specialises in sensory sensitivities – this is usually an occupational therapist. They may be able to do an assessment of your child's particular needs and suggest an appropriate way forward. If this is not an option, then the following strategies could be tried meanwhile:

- Increase gradually the level of touch using a gentle approach to gauge if they prefer a firmer cuddle or a gentler one. It may be that they prefer a very "light" cuddle. Try holding hands as a starting point

- Play fun games to encourage 1:1 social interaction and joint attention, but without the need to cuddle – please don't insist on cuddles if they are expressing a real dislike for having them

Figure 4.12

Sensory sensitivities – tactile hyposensitivity – (seeking touch)

What	Possible reasons why
Holds others in a tight grip	Tactile hyposensitivity
How you might be able to help	

- Give opportunities for deep-pressure activities – an occupational therapist might be able to offer some advice on which ones would be suitable for particular age groups. These activities should provide the appropriate sensory feedback that your child is seeking in a more appropriate way

- At bedtime, try baby sleeping bags or traditional "swaddling" techniques with a baby blanket

- For older children under the age of 5, try tight-fitting pyjamas with cuffs on arms and legs. You could also try to use sheets and blankets in bed that are tucked in to fit snugly

- Play games that involve touch such as rough and tumble, "people" games such as "ring a ring o' roses"

- If they are grabbing at others, try saying their name and then "hands down". Then redirect them to an object that will give the same sensory tactile feedback, e.g., "Koosh" ball, Play-Doh or Plasticine

Figure 4.13

Sensory sensitivities - olfactory hypersensitivity – (avoiding/disliking strong smells)

What	Possible reasons why
1 Gags when food is presented 2 Gags at other smells	Olfactory hypersensitivity

How you might be able to help

1 If your baby is gagging with a bottle feed, speak to your health visitor or doctor to try a different formula feed. As mentioned earlier, it may be that your child is lactose intolerant, and a clinician will be able to assess your child for this:

- Ensure that your child knows *visually* when food is being prepared
- Try to determine which foods are causing the gagging reflex through a process of observation and elimination
- Try foods that are not overly spicy or seasoned
- Try different sized teats

2 As before, try to determine which particular smells are causing this – it could be some of the following:

- Perfume/aftershave – avoid wearing or change the one used
- Deodorant – change to a roll-on rather than spray deodorant (spray will linger in the air for longer)
- Shampoo or conditioner – trial and error to see which one is better received
- Soap – try non-perfumed soap
- Toothpaste – there are some brands available that do not have a taste/smell
- Laundry detergent or fabric softener – as above
- Air fresheners – try eliminating the use of these to gauge the effect
- Furniture polish – try spraying polish at night when your child is asleep
- Household cleaning detergent – try different ones to determine the effect

Figure 4.14

Sensory sensitivities – olfactory hyposensitivity – (seeking/liking strong smells)

What	Possible reasons why
1 Sniffs at people	1 This could be a way to identify the person through their scent
2 Smells/smears own faeces	2 Some autistic children may smear their faeces to gain sensory feedback – both tactile and olfactory senses could be involved
How you might be able to help	

1 Allow your child to sniff at people's wrists if this is something that they are seeking to do – this is more appropriate that sniffing them in other parts of the body . . .

- Redirect them to scented Play-Doh (this can be a good alternative to sniffing at other people
- Provide "scratch and sniff" books when reading stories
- Where possible, incorporate their favourite smells into their everyday experiences

2 When changing your child's nappy (diaper), encourage them to hold a ball of scented Play-Doh (as long as it won't be eaten by them) or a toy that has been washed in a smell that they enjoy:

- If they are using the toilet independently, but putting their hands down the toilet to retrieve faeces, give them something with a pleasant smell to hold while they are seated on the toilet as an alternative. It may be that they prefer a spinning, light-up toy to watch as they defecate – this will also help to distract them from exploring their faeces

Figure 4.15

Sensory sensitivities – gustatory hypersensitivity – (avoiding/disliking tasting items)

What	Possible reasons why
1 Gags at food	Hypersensitivity to olfactory and gustatory sense
2 Will only eat the same foods and be reluctant to try new ones	Autism – restricted and repetitive patterns of behaviour and interests (this explains the disliking of changes)
	Sensory sensitivities to texture, taste, temperature, or smell
How you might be able to help	

1 See strategies for olfactory hypersensitivity; perhaps it is the temperature of the food – some autistic children prefer cold food, while others prefer hot. Observe their reaction to both hot and cold food to determine if there is a preference

2 First point to make is that if you have any concerns about your child's diet or nutritional intake, please consult your doctor who can refer your child to a dietician who may give specific advice and reassurance. Below are some strategies to encourage your child to try some new foods. The general rule is not to force your child to eat or even to highlight the food to them – this could cause further distress for your child:

- Have little amounts of the food you are trying to introduce available just to be looked at initially. The next step is for the food item to be touched, followed by your child putting it on their plate, smelling it, licking it, and then putting it into their mouth to bite it, chew it, and swallow it. It could take months for these steps to be completed, so patience is key (see autism.org.uk)

Figure 4.16

- Try playing with different textures of food, e.g. broken biscuits, wet pasta, if the texture of the new food is preventing their attempt to try it

- Perhaps having the different foods "touch one another" on the plate is unpleasant for your child – maybe moving the different foods apart on the plate might help, or try a plate that has different sections for food items

- Sometimes having a change of brand can be unsettling for autistic children, so keeping to the same brand can be helpful with this. If your child will only eat chicken nuggets from a well-known food outlet with arches, then perhaps using the same packaging might help to disguise home-made ones. Don't be surprised, however, if they can easily discern the difference

Figure 4.16 (Continued)

Sensory sensitivities – gustatory hyposensitivity – (seeking)

What	Possible reasons why
1 **Overfilling mouth with food**	1 Perhaps they may not have an awareness that their mouth has food in it unless it is full
2 **Bites others**	2 There could be many reasons for this including oral hyposensitivity – biting to gain sensory feedback
3 **Communication differences**	3 It could also be because there is little in the way of speech and understanding to communicate their needs, so, for example, if your child is biting others to gain a toy that they would like, it could be easier for them to do that to get it, rather than use speech
How you might be able to help	

1 Seek advice from a speech and language therapist who may be able to offer expert advice and guidance on this issue. In the meantime, the following strategies may help:

- Closely observe your child when eating to avoid incidents of choking
- Give only small amounts of food at a time to avoid over "packing"
- Encourage your child to take small sips of water in between bites

Figure 4.17

2 If oral hyposensitivity is the issue, then the following may help:

- Provide a teething ring, or if the child is slightly older, "chewellery" – there are many forms of this available for different age groups – if you type "chewellery" into an internet search engine, you will find many different retail outlets that sell these items. These objects can provide the sensory feedback that is more appropriate for their needs – better than biting others

3 If communication is the issue, then the following may help:

- Ask others to approach your child face on – this will avoid any sudden surprises that could lead to their biting in response to being startled

- Monitor instances when biting occurs to check if there is a pattern. If it is because of differences in social interactions like sharing or turn taking, then it is important to teach about these

Figure 4.17 (Continued)

Sensory sensitivities – proprioception hypersensitivity – (avoiding feedback)

What	Possible reasons why
1 Bumps into objects, appears awkward in movements	1 Possible co-ordination difficulties, eye sight
2 Difficulties with using fine motor skills, e.g., using cutlery	2 Hand-eye co-ordination difficulties, social understanding of using cutlery. It might not make sense to some autistic children that we use cutlery – it is easier for some children to use their hands, and using cutlery is a skill that needs taught to every child

How you might be able to help

1 Seek advice from an occupational therapist if you have real concerns about your child's ability with movements. In the meantime, this may help:

- Ensure that areas are clutter (and obstacle) free

- Clearly define areas and floor space. For some autistic children, it can be helpful to mark out areas where there are different levels of flooring by using coloured tape to denote them

- It is a good idea to have your child's eye sight checked to rule out vision problems as a cause of their bumping into objects

2 There are specially adapted knives, forks, and spoons available for children who find it difficult to use conventional cutlery. It is advisable to begin with a spoon and then once the use of this is mastered, progress to a fork. If you type "adaptive cutlery autism" into an internet search engine, you should find all the information you need:

- Provide fun fine motor skills activities including threading large beads, posting coins into a piggy bank (with very close supervision), using Play-Doh, popping bubble wrap, etc. All of these with adult supervision due to potential choking hazards, especially if items are "mouthed" by your child

Figure 4.18

Sensory sensitivities – proprioception hyposensitivity – (seeking proprioceptive feedback)

What	Possible reasons why
Bouncing or bangs self on the floor	Autism – many autistic people experience the senses differently (autism.org.uk). These actions can be distressing to witness, but they may be giving the child the sensory feedback they are seeking
How you might be able to help	

It is important to say that if your child is banging their head on a consistent basis, it is best to seek medical advice about this. Speak to an occupational therapist who can advise on "deep-pressure" activities. These can help to give the feedback that is being sought. An occupational therapist can determine what is the right course of action for your child's particular circumstances. If they are bouncing their body on the floor, consider trying some of the following:

- Redirect this sensory seeking action to a more appropriate and safer one such as using a trampoline, or placing a cushion underneath the child, or playing "people games" such as "horsey, horsey" that involves a bouncing action on the adult's knee rather than a hard floor

- Take your child to a soft play facility – better to go at quieter times of the day

- Try gentle massage on the body – this may be enough to give the feedback that your child is seeking, but again, in a safer way

- If the banging of the head is severe, the occupational therapist may suggest the wearing of a padded helmet to protect the skull

- It is important to stress that if your child is preverbal, they may be experiencing pain in their head, and this may be the way they are trying to communicate this. Again, seek medical advice if you are unsure

Figure 4.19

Sensory sensitivities – vestibular hypersensitivity – (avoiding vestibular feedback)

What	Possible reasons why
1 Dislikes baby swings/jumpers 2 Avoids playground equipment 3 Motion sickness while travelling	Vestibular hypersensitivity
How you might be able to help	

1 Avoid the use of toys where motion is involved, e.g., baby swings and "jumpers". Instead, try to give toys that can be played with while seated or lying down

2 Observe which playground equipment your child avoids; it may be that the roundabout or swings give too much vestibular feedback, so perhaps try to encourage them to play with equipment with which they can exercise some degree of control, e.g., come down a slide with you holding them initially for the last part of the slide and gradually increasing the amount of the slide being used (still being held by you). I would do this very slowly initially and smile at them while doing it – if it appears fun to you, it may not be as intimidating for them to experience it

3 Where possible, have your child placed in the middle seat of your car so that they have a forward facing view while travelling. *This is not advisable for babies*

- Try to keep the journey as smooth as possible – large, sudden movements can upset the vestibular system

- Ensure straps in the car seat or buggy are snugly fitted – giving them extra security

- Try placing a solid object underneath their feet while travelling in the car

- Use a "buggy board" when your child is accompanying their younger sibling in a pram

Figure 4.20

Sensory sensitivities – vestibular hyposensitivity – (seeking vestibular feedback)

What	Possible reasons why
1 Continually running and spinning	Vestibular hyposensitivity
2 Climbing onto high surfaces	
How you might be able to help	

1 Encourage your child to walk rather than run; the following may help:

- Take their hand, or have them wear a backpack with a strap attached, that you can hold from behind. Or use a child's harness while out and about and especially near roads (not having an awareness of road safety may be an issue)

- Encourage the release of energy through regular bursts of physical play, e.g., using tricycles, scooters or participating in ring games such as "ring a ring o' roses". This ring game involves lots of fast, spinning movements

- Use a trampoline to eliminate excess energy

- Check sugar intake in your child's diet – see a dietician's advice on dietary issues

- Check "E" numbers in food labels – this can also cause some children to be very active (www.nhs.uk/conditions/food-colours-and-hyperactivity/)

2 This can be very frightening for parents whose children may surprise them by climbing onto extremely high surfaces that parents thought were inaccessible to their child. The following strategies may help with this sensory seeking action:

- Where possible, avoid allowing access to higher surfaces by removing stools, chairs near cupboards in the kitchen, and have locks placed on cupboard doors

Figure 4.21

- Provide alternatives to climbing onto furniture, e.g., climbing frame in garden or soft play experiences
- Give opportunities to move legs to music or during ring games – this movement may give the sensory feedback being sought, but without the element of danger
- Encourage your child to "climb" onto you and then flip them over (safely!)
- Play "rough and tumble" games for vestibular feedback

Figure 4.21 (Continued)

Sensory sensitivities – interoception hypersensitivity – (oversensitivity)

What	Possible reasons why
1 Overeating or putting too much food into mouth	1 Body cannot tell when it is full
2 Always appearing to be cold – wanting to add extra layers of clothing	2 Difficulty with body regulating temperature

How you might be able to help
1 Overfilling the mouth can present as a choking hazard, so it is important to seek help with this and closely observe them at meal times. A speech and language therapist can provide an eating and drinking plan to help. It is best to seek advice from a qualified medical professional such as your child's health visitor or doctor for more advice about this. It is also a good idea to limit the amount of food you put on your child's plate at any one time. It can also help to cut food into smaller pieces before presenting it to them. Please be careful that the pieces are not cut so small that they present as a choking hazard to your child
2 Check their body temperature with a thermometer to ensure that their body is not too cold

Figure 4.22

Sensory sensitivities – interoception hyposensitivity – (under-sensitivity)

What	Possible reasons why
1 Not appearing to be hungry or thirsty	1 Body cannot tell when it needs food or water
2 Always appearing to be hot – unwilling to remove layers of clothing	2 Difficulty with body knowing when it is too hot

How you might be able to help
1 • Monitor actual food and drink intake throughout the day and speak with your doctor or health visitor if you feel that they are not getting enough nutrients or if they are not eating or drinking enough • Provide regular meals at predictable times throughout the day to establish a regular pattern for your child of when they should be eating and drinking • Use food items, photographs, or visuals to give notice to your child when it is time to eat 2 • Provide looser fitting, cotton layers that don't trap as much heat as synthetic materials • Monitor their temperature with a "remote" thermometer (one you point at the forehead)

Figure 4.23

Going on visits (supermarket)

What	Possible reasons why
Upset at the mention of going on trips or refusal to participate in them	There could be a number of reasons why this may be upsetting for your child including the following: 1 Sensory sensitivity to noise 2 Sensory sensitivity to too much visual stimuli 3 Unpredictable element – perhaps it is a sudden or unexpected trip that they were not anticipating 4 They may worry that they are not coming back home after the trip 5 The journey itself will make them feel unwell – car sickness, perhaps 6 Different route taken on the journey 7 Unhappy association with a particular place, e.g., last time this particular place was mentioned, they had a meltdown
How you might be able to help	

1

- Go at a quieter time, e.g., to the supermarket – there are times in the day when fewer people will go shopping, and there will be, as a consequence, less noise
- Provide ear defenders to nullify the noise
- Encourage your child to wear a hat or their hood up if it helps to block out some of the noise

Figure 4.24

2

- Provide an alternative visual distraction that your child enjoys, e.g., spinning light wand or "Koosh" light-up ball
- If your child tolerates wearing a hat, provide them with one that will cover most of their vision, e.g., a baseball cap to block out visual stimuli
- Allow your child to wear sunglasses indoors. This can help to block out some of the glare from lights in shops

3

- Use photographs of the places you will be visiting and show these in advance to give your child time to process where they will be going, keeping your words simple, e.g., "Johnny, shopping" rather than "Johnny, we're going to go shopping now so let's get ready"

4

- Giving predictability by saying "shopping, then home" showing a photograph of each event. When shopping is finished, show the photograph of home – making sure you go straight home and not via a detour

5

- Keep them occupied on the journey with a favourite toy/ game or thing they have to do, e.g., "let's count the trees on the way"

6

- Try to stick to the same route each time; this can provide predictability

7

- If you can, avoid places with which your child has formed a negative association with a particular incident, e.g., if your child has had a meltdown in one supermarket, try changing to a different one. Be sure to give them plenty of notice beforehand; perhaps look at this new supermarket online to make them familiar with it

Figure 4.24 (Continued)

Going on visits (hairdresser)

What	Possible reasons why
Dislikes haircuts	Autism – tactile hypersensitivity, but could also include auditory and visual hypersensitivity

How you might be able to help

In my experience working with young autistic children, this can be a real problem for families, and parents may feel that they have no choice but to resort to cutting their own child's hair. Hopefully some of these strategies may help to avoid the need for this:

- Visit a quiet hair salon during quiet times. Best not to change hairdressers – the exception to this would be if your child has been really upset or distressed in a particular hair salon on a previous occasion – they may then associate that location with that experience and not want to go there, as the connection to that place is not good for them

- Try to keep to the same routine on each visit – giving plenty of notice to your child that you are going to visit

- Give a familiar and enjoyable toy as a treat to play with when they are on the hairdressing chair. This could be a favourite sensory toy such as a light-up wand or a fidget toy. You may even want to consider giving a food treat too – their favourite snack to eat. The more pleasant the experience, the more they may associate a visit there as a good thing that they enjoy doing and will want to repeat in the future

- Ask the hairdresser to use scissors instead of loud buzzing clippers

- It might be an idea to bring the shampoo your child is familiar with using, to give some consistency

Figure 4.25

- Ask the hairdresser to spray the hair wet rather than wash the hair in a basin if they really don't like having this done. Perhaps a game can be made of spraying the hair – hairdresser having a spray – your child having a spray

- Consider whether your child might prefer to have their hair gently towel dried rather than use the hairdryer if they have hypersensitivity to the sound. They may even prefer to dry their own hair with the towel

- Give lots of praise (if your child can cope with lots of praise) when they have had their hair cut

- Don't put any further demands on your child that day, e.g., avoid going shopping or visiting relatives to show them the new haircut

Figure 4.25 (Continued)

Attending medical appointments

What	Possible reasons why
Attending a dental appointment	Autism – tactile hypersensitivity, but could also include auditory and visual hypersensitivity

How you might be able to help

This can often be a very traumatic experience for some autistic children and their families. As with all the strategies in this book, there is no "one size fits all" approach as each individual autistic child is different, and their sensory experiences are therefore different. Listed here are some strategies that may help should your child find visiting the dentist an unsettling experience.

Preparation *before* the visit:

- If you can, try to source a dentist who has knowledge and experience of autism

- Arrange the appointment for a less busy time – ask your dentist when is best

- Prepare them for the visit by reading lots of stories about "going to the dentist" – see suggested reading at the end of this chapter

- Pretend play "at the dentist" – this gives an opportunity for your child to open their mouth and for you to pretend to be looking inside with a toy dental implement – from a doctor's play set. This can be done in front of a mirror so that they can see what you see

- Count your child's teeth in front of the mirror

- Talk about what the purposes of our teeth, and how it is important to look after them. Please bear in mind how much information your child is able to process – remember to keep your words short and simple to aid their understanding

Figure 4.26

- Take turns at being the dentist with your child
- If your dental surgery has a website, then show this to your child to make them familiar with the layout and the dentist (if their picture is on it, if not, perhaps you could ask your dentist if you could take a photograph of them in their practice). You can highlight to them the special chair for them to sit in while the dentist is looking in their mouth
- If you have a photograph of the dentist, then put this on the day of the calendar when you will be taking your child and cross off the days until then, so that they know when this will happen

On the *day of the visit*:

- On the first visit, try to keep it brief – a quick check up to get them used to the environment and sitting in the big chair
- Bring along something that you know your child will love, e.g., small sensory toy or electronic game. This can be given when they sit in the chair. If they don't sit in the chair, then perhaps the dentist can come down to their level to examine them?
- A word of caution, before your child sits in the chair, let them see how it can move up and down – this may either intrigue them, or it may put them off wanting to sit in it at all
- The bright light that dentists usually shine above your head may be too intense and bright for your child, so perhaps the dentist could use a handheld light instead? Or perhaps your child could wear sunglasses?
- It's always advisable for medical practitioners including dentists to say what they are going to do in advance – no sudden surprises! – giving plenty of time to prepare
- If, on subsequent visits, there are to be any drills or loud equipment being used, it is a good idea (if your child can cope with headphones), to play favourite songs or use ear defenders to block out the noise completely

Figure 4.26 (Continued)

Attending medical appointments

What	Possible reasons why
Attending an appointment at the doctor	Autism – tactile hypersensitivity, but could also include auditory and visual hypersensitivity

How you might be able to help	

As with dental appointments, preparation for the visit is key. Visiting the doctor can be a frightening experience for young autistic children, so lots of practice at pretend playing doctors with teddies and with each other may help to give some insight into what your child might expect at the doctor's surgery

Preparation *before* the visit:

The strategies suggested in the dental visit preparation would work here too, but you might also want to consider the following:

- Practise taking temperatures with a real thermometer – a forehead one is good as it is not as invasive as one that is put into the mouth

- Pretend play could also include practising lying on the examination couch (your couch or their bed at home)

- Pretend play could include cleaning a wound, bandaging a wound, or putting on a plaster. The pretend play cannot cover all possible, individual reasons why your child may need to visit the doctor, but it may help

- As with the dental visit, read stories about going to the doctor – this can help to explain to your child why they may need to go there

On the *day of the visit*:

- Try not to show your anxiety about how they may respond to the visit – they may sense this and respond in the same way

- As with the dental visit, try to keep the first visit as brief as possible

- Bring along a favourite toy or game to keep them occupied while the doctor is examining them

Figure 4.27

Recommended reading

[See also References for more information.]

- *The Potty Journey*
- *Going to the Doctor*
- *Going to the Dentist*

The next section is aimed at children aged between 5 and 12 years – primary (elementary) school-aged autistic children. As mentioned previously, many of the strategies in this section can "cross over" to the younger age group, and, indeed, some can "cross over" into the next age group, so please bear this in mind.

It is also important to note that autism is a lifelong condition, and, as such, many of these strategies will be useful beyond the teenage years (discussed in Part 3 of this chapter).

Let's look now at how you can support your autistic child aged between 5 and 12.

PART 2 CHILDREN AGED BETWEEN 5 AND 12

This can be a difficult age for many autistic children as it can often be their first experience of attending formal education, which can be challenging for them. With this in mind, I have added a section on how best to prepare your child for their first school visit – in the "visits" section towards the end of this part of the chapter.

If there are any sections where similar strategies to those suggested in Part 1 would apply in this age group, it will state "See Part 1 strategies" in the "How you might be able to help" section. This is done to avoid any duplication.

It is important to mention again that not all autistic children aged between 5 and 12 will experience these differences and require strategies to support them. If, however, you are looking for some help for this age group, then the following may be useful.

Social communication and interaction

What	Possible reasons why
Not using words to communicate	Many autistic children may be late to speak, some may never speak, while others may speak from an early age
How you might be able to help	

If your child is still not speaking by the age of 5, I would strongly urge you to seek advice and support from a speech and language therapist who may help

Meanwhile, please refer to Part 1 strategies for some additional ideas

Figure 4.28

Social communication and interaction

What	Possible reasons why
Making loud vocalisations – screaming/ shouting	1 Pain
	2 Sensory sensitivities
	3 Changes to routines
How you might be able to help	

1 It can be difficult for an autistic child to verbalise what and where their pain may be. It can help to ask "show me your 'ouch!'". If they are not responding to this, try to have a large drawing of a child's body and say "show me where it hurts", while you point, "does it hurt here? Or here?" Please be mindful that some autistic children can be quite literal, and so will not point to a picture as that is not where *their* pain is . . . As always, however, if your child is displaying any signs of illness, please consult with a medical professional and explain to them that your child is autistic

2 Be a sensory "detective" and try to establish if there is a pattern – if it is a hearing issue, then using ear defenders may help. Sometimes autistic children with hypersensitivity to sound can themselves be very loud to drown out the sounds they are hearing. Very often people say to me "but he is the loudest child in the room, so how can he be hypersensitive to sounds?" The simple answer is that they are *in control* of what noise they are making, so this is predictable, whereas loud sounds that can happen out of their control, e.g., a balloon popping or dog barking, are not predictable, and therefore can be very stressful for them

3 See Part 1 for additional strategies

Figure 4.29

Social communication and interaction

What	Possible reasons why
Doesn't respond to others verbally, e.g., in conversations or to verbal requests	1 Perhaps doesn't know that the person is talking directly to them 2 Auditory hypersensitivity – may have their hands over their ears 3 Difficulty in processing information given verbally 4 Too many demands being placed upon them
How you might be able to help	

1 Say your child's name first to gain their attention – they may still not look at you, but this does not mean that they are not listening to you

2 Reduce background noise, e.g., if the television is playing in the same room, this may be too distracting for them

3 Give at least 20 seconds for your child to process any verbal requests or information – it may seem like a long wait, but it can help autistic children to make sense of what is being asked if they are given time to do so. Speaking slowly and keeping words to a minimum will also help with this

4 Try to avoid asking your child to look at you while they are listening – they may not be able to do both at the same time

Figure 4.30

Social communication and interaction

What	Possible reasons why
Being very literal in interpreting words and phrases. For example, "it's raining cats and dogs"	Autism – social communication and interaction differences

How you might be able to help

- Explain to your child that words that are *spelled the same* can have different meanings (homonyms), e.g., "tear" can mean what you shed when you cry, and the action of ripping. Also explain also that words that *sound the same* (homophones) can be spelled differently, e.g., right and write. This is something that could cause confusion, but could help make sense of phrases such as "batting your eyelashes"

- Teach them about idioms of speech and how many of them seem silly, e.g., "it's raining cats and dogs" simply means it's raining heavily or "dog tired" means you are *really* tired

- Think of how many words your child knows that mean the same thing, e.g., pretty, beautiful, gorgeous, lovely etc. This will help your child to appreciate that one word does not just refer to one thing, e.g., you can use many different words to describe the same thing

- Teach about collective nouns, e.g., gulls and magpies can be called these names, but they can also be called "birds". This will also help to generalise meaning, e.g., dolls, teddies, pretend cars are all "toys", so teach them this word and ask if they can think of other toys that could be included within this group

Figure 4.31

71

Social communication and interaction

What	Possible reasons why
1 **Speaking with a different accent, usually American or very "posh" English – "received pronunciation" (RP)**	1 This can be seen in some young autistic children – some are very adept too at "switching" accents as they grow. There does not seem to be an explanation at present for why this happens
2 **Speaking at a high or low volume**	2 May be linked to auditory sensitivities

How you might be able to help

1 As long as your autistic child is communicating their needs and choices, this should not matter. If you try to correct your child, they may not see a reason for communicating at all

2 It may be that your child finds it difficult to "filter" out loud noises (that they perceive to be loud) by being louder than the noises to "drown" them out. You can help by using a volume gauge with an arrow pointing to "too loud", "too quiet", or "just right" – this can be represented visually with a green light for "just right", a red light for "too loud", and an amber for "too quiet". When your child is too loud, show them that the arrow is pointing to red, so they need to be quieter, model how quiet you would like them to be using the arrow to demonstrate, and ask them to try this volume. There are some apps that can be used in this way too – if your child responds better to this method

Figure 4.32

Social communication and interaction

What	Possible reasons why
Repeating words or phrases – perhaps from a favourite television show or film out of context (i.e., not in the moment) – like echolalia (see Part 1), but repeating words in this way may occur days/ weeks after the event	1 Delayed echolalia 2 Self-soothing – if stressed (coping mechanism)
How you might be able to help	
1 Again, acknowledge this, as before with echolalia. Perhaps this might be the way that a request to watch that film or television show is being communicated? 2 If repeating television shows or phrases will destress your child, then this should not be discouraged	

Figure 4.33

Social communication and interaction

What	Possible reasons why
Talking at length about their favourite topic or enthusiasm, e.g., dinosaurs, sharks, etc.	1 Enjoyment at being very knowledgeable about their topic of interest and wanting to share this knowledge with someone 2 Having a "script" of what they are going to talk about may give them predictability and therefore comfort 3 Enjoyment in interacting with familiar people
How you might be able to help	

1 Listen to their talk about their favourite topic without interruption (if you interrupt, you may send them "off track" and they may start from the beginning again, and this may upset them)

2 If you know that the talk will be repeated at length, say that you will listen until the big hand on the clock reaches (whatever time suits you) and then the talk should stop. This will help to give them predictability about the duration of their talk

3 Try saying "I've listened to your talk, it's now finished, and so now we are going to talk about/do . . ."

Figure 4.34

Social communication and interaction

What	Possible reasons why
Wanting to make friends but unsure how to begin	Differences in social communication and interaction due to being autistic

How you might be able to help

It is important to say that many autistic children may not want to have a friend – this could be due to the differences mentioned above, but also because of other reasons such as sensory sensitivities, the unpredictable element of other people – not being in control of what others may do or say may be stressful for them. If, however, you feel that your child could cope with having a friend, then the following strategies may help:

- Model some conversation "starters" with a teddy bear/doll as the pretend friend, or use a hand puppet to be the "friend" – this way, the puppet can "respond verbally". These conversation "starters" could include "Hi, I'm . . . Want to play with me?/play with my cars?/play 'tag?'", etc.

- Explain what to say if someone refuses, e.g., "That's ok, maybe another time?"

- Having a "script" like this can be helpful if they are unsure of how to respond

- Invite one or two school classmates over for a "play date" – if they are comfortable with this

- Read stories to your child about friendship, and why friends can be important

- Ask your child if they would like to join a club – it may be a club that would centre around their favourite subject. Ask your child's school if they run after-school clubs and discuss these with your child, perhaps they may want to be part of one. Please don't insist that they join one if they are showing a real aversion to this

Figure 4.35

Sensory sensitivities – auditory (hearing) hypersensitivity – (avoiding)

What	Possible reasons why
Hands over ears	• Auditory hypersensitivity to a variety of stimuli including, for example, a baby's cry, a telephone ringing, a fire bell, a balloon popping, a raised voice, etc. • Too much noise in the environment, e.g., in places where there are crowds of people, e.g., at the swimming pool, in school, at the supermarket, on public transport, or in the cinema • Many autistic adults speak about how they are unable to filter out sounds such as a ticking clock. Many report hearing noises that others cannot hear due to hypersensitivity – this should not be dismissed, but rather, taken seriously

How you might be able to help
• As mentioned in Part 1 – use ear defenders if noises are unbearable for your child. There are some very good ones for children, but if you want something more discreet, then try ear "buds" – be mindful of health and safety, however, especially if your child is still mouthing objects • If your autistic child has a baby brother or sister, avoid them sharing rooms if possible if the baby's crying is too overwhelming for them in terms of noise, pitch, or duration of the crying • Weather permitting, encourage your child to wear a tight fitting hat – this could be worn with the ear defenders if outdoors. Please be mindful of their safety and of potential hazards such as traffic, when their ears are covered • Encourage your child to wear a tight-fitting swimming hat when at the pool

Figure 4.36

- Avoid busy places at peak times
- Use the vacuum cleaner when your child is at school or if they are listening to music on headphones
- Turn the volume down on the television and other electronic devices
- Switch off devices that are not being used
- Avoid fluorescent lighting as these can emit a buzzing sound to some autistic children
- Close windows if it is noisy outside, e.g., when people are mowing their lawns
- Avoid having ticking or chiming clocks if these noises upset your child
- Use door "silencers" to reduce noise when doors are closed – this avoids doors slamming shut
- Rugs on hard floors can also minimise sound quite effectively
- Put pads on chair legs to prevent noise on hard flooring

Figure 4.36 (Continued)

Sensory sensitivities – auditory hyposensitivity – (seeking)

What	Possible reasons why
Making loud noises vocally or by banging on objects	• Seeking auditory feedback. • Being in control of noise that they experience

How you might be able to help

This is a difficult issue for many families who may feel that the child is just being particularly noisy for no reason. The following strategies may help:

- Try to provide a context for the noise making, e.g., using musical instruments or singing

- Use the "distraction technique" – sometimes it can help to shift their focus onto something else, e.g., their special interest

- Use visuals such as "stop" or "quiet voice" to remind them if they are being particularly loud. This will, with all visuals, need to be taught and involve lots of practice

- Provide headphones for playing music – this will give the auditory feedback they are seeking, but avoids the rest of the household being exposed to this

Figure 4.37

Sensory sensitivities – visual hypersensitivity – (avoiding)

What	Possible reasons why
Covering or squinting eyes	Visual hypersensitivity
How you might be able to help	

See Part 1 for strategies, but also consider the following for school:

- If your child tells you that they cover their eyes frequently in school, ask their teacher where they are sitting in class. If they are positioned near to, or facing directly towards a window, this could be too visually stimulating for them

- If your child wears glasses, think about having lenses that automatically (and quickly) adapt to changes in light levels. Speak to an optician about these types of lenses

Figure 4.38

Sensory sensitivities – visual hyposensitivity – (seeking)

What	Possible reasons why
Looking very closely at objects	Visual hyposensitivity
How you might be able to help	

See Part 1 for strategies, but also consider the following for school:

- Visual timetable on their desk if the class visual timetable is too far away to view clearly

Figure 4.39

Sensory sensitivities – tactile hypersensitivity – (avoiding touch)

What	Possible reasons why
Avoiding hugs or close physical interaction with others	For many autistic people, physical touching can be painful for them. There are many instances where objects or people touching their skin can mean sensory overload for them including the following: 1 Being hugged 2 Labels on clothing 3 Water touching their skin while showering

How you might be able to help

1

- If your child experiences a sensory overload with touch, please ask family members not to insist on hugs – ask your child instead how they would like to be greeted, e.g., wave, "air" "hi 5", smile, or the person requesting the hug to hug themselves to show that this is meant for them

2

- Remove labels from clothing if they experience discomfort with them against their skin
- Use a fabric softener when washing their clothes – but be mindful of the scent
- Long-sleeved clothing and full-length trousers can help to minimise skin to skin contact with others who may brush past

3

- A shower cap and goggles may help when they are in the shower
- Try using a very light spray setting in the shower head

Figure 4.40

Sensory sensitivities – tactile hyposensitivity – (seeking touch)

What	Possible reasons why
Being in others' personal space to seek tactile feedback	Not understanding the social rules of personal space and safety
How you might be able to help	

- *Social Story*™ (Gray 2015) about why it is important to respect the personal space of others, and how it makes others feel when their space is encroached, or when they receive an unwanted (and sometimes very tight) hug

- Demonstration of what is appropriate in terms of personal space – your child may not know that approaching a complete stranger to cuddle them is not safe or appropriate. You could explain that a "stranger" is someone that they do not know

- Giving alternatives to seeking tactile feedback such as an object that they can squeeze, e.g., "Koosh" ball, Theraputty™ or fidget toy

Figure 4.41

Sensory sensitivities – olfactory hypersensitivity – (avoiding smells)

What	Possible reasons why
1 Gags when food is presented	1 Olfactory hypersensitivity
2 Gags at other smells	2 Texture or temperature of the food

How you might be able to help
1   • Provide a packed lunch for school if your child gags at the food on offer in school. If your child's school has a weekly menu, then it can help to determine which food they may try/enjoy and which food to avoid   • Ask if your child can sit away from the source of the smell – this is not always possible, but worth asking   • Have a smell that they enjoy sprayed onto a handkerchief that they can sniff, to override the unpleasant smell making them gag   2   See Part 1 for additional strategies   • If your child's teacher is wearing a strong perfume/ aftershave, then the scented handkerchief may help with this too

Figure 4.42

Sensory sensitivities – olfactory hyposensitivity – (seeking smells)

What	Possible reasons why
Smearing faeces	Olfactory hyposensitivity
	Tactile hyposensitivity

How you might be able to help

This can be upsetting to witness for all concerned. It is important to mention, however, that the action itself may not upset your child, but the reactions of *others* may be very upsetting to them. The following strategies may help:

- Try to establish if there is a pattern to when your child is doing this. Is it always after using the toilet? Is it linked to a particular situation, for example, does it happen before going to a place that they find stressful?

- Try not to show a negative reaction when it occurs; remaining calm will help your child

- Provide a substitute for the faeces. There are many different kinds of scented play dough that can provide both the olfactory and tactile feedback that they may be seeking

- If it happens when your child is not in school, e.g., in a public place with you, consider adapted clothing such as back zipped all in one undergarments – available online. These are very difficult for the child to gain access to the "contents" and could preserve their dignity when out and about in the community

- Use a visual timetable to demonstrate the steps needed to use the toilet. This should be within your child's eye line of vision, and be accessible to them, as they will need to turn over each step as it is completed. Toileting visual schedules are available online

Figure 4.43

Sensory sensitivities – gustatory hypersensitivity – (avoiding/disliking tasting items)

What	Possible reasons why
Eating a self-selected and limiting diet	Gustatory hypersensitivity due to texture, temperature, location of food on the plate

How you might be able to help

It is important to say that if your child only eats a small and self-selected type of food, e.g., breaded items such as chicken nuggets or smooth foods such as yoghurts, then it is important to consult a dietician who will offer specialist advice on your child's specific preferences and possible dietary supplements should these be required. Please do not be under the assumption that your child is being a "fussy eater", this is simply not the case. Gustatory hypersensitivity is common with autistic children and adults, and should never be compared to "picky eating". The following strategies may help a child who has a real aversion to specific foods:

- Try new foodstuffs gradually and *not* discreetly – please make it obvious that you're introducing new items. If it is vegetables you want to introduce, place only one of each on the plate and encourage your child to touch it initially, lick it, and, if they are able to, put it in their mouth. Please do not insist on its being eaten at this stage, it is early days, and they may never eat it. Also, please *do not insist* that they touch it or lick it – they may not yet be ready for this either

- Encourage new foods by using their favourite character as a role model. For example, "Batman loves to eat peas"

- There are plates available that are segmented into different sections. This is especially helpful if your child has an aversion to different food items touching one another on the plate

- Provide a packed lunch for your child in school if they cannot eat what is on the lunch menu

Figure 4.44

Sensory sensitivities – gustatory hyposensitivity – (seeking)

What	Possible reasons why
Putting inedible items into the mouth, e.g., stones, earth, grass, leaves, etc.	This is referred to as "Pica" Seeking oral sensory feedback

How you might be able to help

"Pica" can be a choking hazard, so it is important to let those involved with your child know that they may attempt to put inedible items into their mouth. They can then risk assess how best to support your child with this. Other ways to help can include the following:

- Provide a chewing alternative to the inedible items. There are many different types of "chewellery" available online including ones worn around the wrist or neck and handheld ones

- *Social Story*™ to explain how we use our mouths: for eating food, for smiling, for talking

- Discuss food/non-food items and have your child sort them into eating/not for eating groups

- Provide small, healthy snacking substitutes if your child attempts to eat an inedible item

Figure 4.45

Sensory sensitivities – proprioception hypersensitivity – (avoiding feedback)

What	Possible reasons why
Fatigues easily	Proprioception hypersensitivity can cause children to become tired easily. It can also have an effect on your child's fine motor skills and with their ability to follow steps in a sequence, e.g., tying shoelaces. Some gross motor skills such as learning dance steps or exercise moves can also be impacted
How you might be able to help	

It is important to rule out other factors that may be causing your child to be easily fatigued. With this in mind, please seek out medical assistance to reassure you that there is not another explanation for your child's fatigue.

Practical strategies for fatigue due to proprioception hypersensitivity are as follows:

- Break down tasks and activities into manageable "chunks"
- Use visuals to help with sequencing events or tasks. Words disappear, but images remain . . .
- Give time for your child to process information before moving onto the next instruction
- Provide rest times if your child is too tired. For example, your child may not have the energy to participate in physical activity when they come home from school
- Establish a good bedtime routine to ensure that your child is getting plenty of sleep

Figure 4.46

Sensory sensitivities – proprioception hyposensitivity – (seeking feedback)

What	Possible reasons why
High energy – running, climbing, jumping	Seeking proprioceptive feedback

How you might be able to help
<ul><li>Provide "heavy work" activities such as housework: vacuuming (if noise is tolerated), laundry work, and cleaning</li><li>Wall "push-ups" standing facing the wall, pushing against it ten times</li><li>Provide a backpack containing some heavy items (not too heavy!) to give weighted feedback when out and about</li><li>Ask your child to carry some of your shopping (if not too heavy!)</li><li>Ask your child to push the shopping trolley</li><li>Position your child's bed against a wall to allow them to squeeze their body against the wall and the bed</li><li>Provide tight-fitting clothing underneath their regular clothes</li></ul>

Figure 4.47

Sensory sensitivities – vestibular hypersensitivity – (avoiding feedback)

What	Possible reasons why
Fear of activities involving heights or that require balance	Vestibular hypersensitivity can mean that some autistic children have an intense fear of escalators, swings, spinning movements, and going on vehicle journeys
How you might be able to help	

It is important again, to rule out any problems with balance and, in particular, the inner ear. A visit to an audiologist will determine this.

Here are some strategies you can try if the problem is connected to the vestibular sense:

See Part 1 for additional strategies, but also try to:

- Use a footstool when seated to give a sense of "grounding"
- Hold your child's hand when ascending/descending escalators and stairs to give reassurance. Encourage them to hold on to the handrail for extra security
- Incorporate gentle swinging movements into "rough and tumble" play. If your child cannot cope with this, then please do not pursue any further
- Ensure that the seatbelt is a snug fit when travelling in the car. This may give them stability and security
- Count out how long it takes to travel from the bottom to the top of the escalator. This works particularly well if your child has an interest in numbers
- Use "ready, steady, go" or "3-2-1-go" when putting their foot onto the first step of the escalator – giving a "countdown" such as this can better prepare your child for it

Figure 4.48

Sensory sensitivities – vestibular hyposensitivity – (seeking feedback)

What	Possible reasons why
Constant movement	Seeking vestibular feedback
How you might be able to help	

- Use a "wobble" or "move 'n' sit" cushion (with raised bumps) to give vestibular feedback while seated. This could also be helpful for use in your child's school

- Provide play resources that encourage movement such as a trampoline or skipping ropes

- Use timers to try to limit the amount of time being spent on movement activities

- Encourage your child to take up a physical hobby such as martial arts club, dance class, or gym activities to eliminate excess energy

Figure 4.49

Sensory sensitivities – interoception hypersensitivity – (oversensitivity)

What	Possible reasons why
1 Overeating or putting too much food into mouth	1 Body cannot tell when it is full
2 Always appearing to be cold – wanting to add extra layers of clothing	2 Difficulty with body regulating temperature

How you might be able to help

1

- As mentioned in Part 1, overfilling the mouth can present as a choking hazard, so it is important to seek help with this and closely observe them at meal times. A speech and language therapist can provide an eating and drinking plan to help, and it is best to seek advice from a qualified medical professional, such as your child's health visitor or doctor for more advice about this. It is a good idea to limit the amount of food you put on your child's plate at any one time

- A *Social Story*™ (Gray 2015) can often help to explain about choking hazards due to overfilling the mouth

- "Comic strip conversations" can also help to explain why you are concerned about this (autism.org.uk)

- Seek advice from a dietician or health professional if you feel that your child is eating too much and you are concerned about their health

2

- Depending on your child's level of understanding, either you use a forehead thermometer on them to determine their temperature, or ask them to do this by themselves (this can give them a greater degree of control)

- Provide loose layers of clothing – cotton is cooler than synthetic fabrics.

- If your child is cold in class, ask their teacher where they are sitting in relation to heating. Perhaps sitting nearer to the radiator, or away from draughts may help

- Consult your doctor to determine if there is anything that they can recommend

Figure 4.50

Sensory sensitivities – interoception hyposensitivity – (under-sensitivity)

What	Possible reasons why
1 Not appearing to be hungry or thirsty	1 Body cannot tell when it needs food or water
2 Always appearing to be hot – unwilling to remove layers of clothing	2 Difficulty with body knowing when it is too hot

How you might be able to help

See Part 1 for additional strategies, but also consider the following:

- Involve your child in the preparation of food. Begin this by preparing their favourite meal. Often, this can help to give a sense of ownership

- Use visuals such as photographs to explain step by step what they must do to prepare the food

- Use a "first and then" board: "first try x" (food that they have not tried before), "then have y" (favourite food)

- If there are tactile sensitivities with food, then encourage glove wearing in preparation of the food

Figure 4.51

Going on visits (supermarket)

What	Possible reasons why
Upset at the mention of trips or refusal to participate	There could be a number of reasons why this may be upsetting for your child including the following: 1 Sensory sensitivity to noise 2 Sensory sensitivity to too much visual stimuli 3 Unpredictable element – perhaps it is a sudden or unexpected trip that they were not anticipating 4 They may worry that they are not coming back home after the trip 5 The journey itself will make them feel unwell – car sickness, perhaps 6 Different route taken on the journey 7 Unhappy association with a particular place, e.g., last time this particular place was mentioned, they had a meltdown
How you might be able to help	

1

- Go at a quieter time, e.g., to the supermarket – there are times in the day when fewer people will go shopping, and there will be, as a consequence, less noise
- Provide ear defenders to nullify the noise or music played through headphones
- Encourage your child to wear a hat or their hood up if it helps to block out some of the noise

2

- Provide an alternative visual distraction that your child enjoys, e.g., spinning light wand or "Koosh" light-up ball

Figure 4.52

- If your child tolerates wearing a hat, provide them with one that will cover most of their vision, e.g., a baseball cap to block out visual stimuli
- Allow your child to wear sunglasses indoors. This can help to block out some of the glare from lights in shops
- Give your child a list of items to buy – this will give visual *purpose* to the visit and avert their gaze away from the visual stimuli that causes upset to them

3

- Use photographs of the places you will be visiting and show these in advance to give your child time to process where they will be going, keeping your words simple, e.g., "Johnny, shopping" rather than "Johnny, we're going to go shopping now so let's get ready"

4

- Provide predictability by saying "shopping, then home" showing a photograph of each event. When shopping is finished, show the photograph of home – making sure you go straight home and not via a detour

5

- Keep them occupied on the journey with a favourite toy/ game or thing they have to do, e.g., "let's count the trees on the way"
- Take a favourite story book to look at during the journey

6

- Try to stick to the same route each time, if it is predictable

7

- Avoid places, if possible, where your child has formed a negative association with a particular incident, e.g., if your child has had a meltdown in one supermarket, try changing to a different one. Be sure to give them plenty of notice beforehand, perhaps look at this new supermarket online to make them familiar with it

Figure 4.52 (Continued)

Going on visits (hairdresser)

What	Possible reasons why
Dislikes haircuts	See Part 1

How you might be able to help

See Part 1 for additional strategies, but also try the following:

- Provide lots of advance notice of the visit – this can be done by crossing off the days until the visit on a month-to-view calendar. The hairdresser visit can be circled

- Ensure that the hairdresser knows that your child is autistic, and may be a little overwhelmed at visiting

- Choose a quiet appointment time to visit

- Read this to your child on the day before the visit:

"Each day your hair grows a little longer. Sometimes it needs to be cut. An adult may say, 'Time for a haircut.' This means that your hair needs to be shorter. We know when your hair is getting too long and will take you to the hairdresser to have it cut. Tomorrow, you are going to have a haircut"

If your child is able to read, give them this "script" for what to do at the hair salon

Here are the steps I need to follow to be a winner at getting my hair cut:

1 Walk into the hairdressers with Mum or Dad

2 Sit in the chair

3 The hairdresser will put a cape over my shoulders. This will keep hair from going on to my clothes. It is safe to wear a cape

Figure 4.53

4 Sit still and listen to what the hairdresser tells me to do. I might have water sprayed on my hair – this will help the hairdresser to cut my hair and it won't hurt me. I can ask for a small towel to cover my eyes if I don't like water being sprayed near me

5 Wait for the hairdresser to cut my hair. They may use scissors or a clipper that cuts hair very short, it makes a buzzing sound, but the scissors and clipper won't hurt me

6 The hairdresser might use a hairdryer that can be noisy, but it also, won't hurt me

7 The hairdresser will take the cape off. This means my haircut is finished

8 Mum or Dad pays money for my haircut

9 Mum or Dad will tell me "you are a winner" for having my hair cut

10 I will leave the hairdressers. Everyone will be happy

Figure 4.53 (Continued)

Attending medical appointments

What	Possible reasons why
Visiting the dentist	Autism – tactile hypersensitivity, but could also include auditory and visual hypersensitivity

How you might be able to help
See Part 1 for additional strategies, but also consider the following: • A *Social Story*™ about why it is important to visit the dentist • "First and then" board: "first dentist, then . . ." (whatever would be a treat for your child; this may be a trip to the cinema, or a visit to the park) A child's baby teeth usually begin to become loose and fall out around the age of 6, so it is important to explain why this is: the bigger teeth are pushing out the smaller ones as the child is growing. A sudden loss of a tooth might be very upsetting for an autistic child, and they may not appreciate why this is happening. This is a good time to talk about the "tooth fairy", and there are lots of good books and stories about this to read to your child when this happens

Figure 4.54

Attending medical appointments

What	Possible reasons why
Visiting the doctor	Autism – tactile hypersensitivity, but could also include auditory and visual hypersensitivity

How you might be able to help

See Part 1 for additional strategies, but also consider the following:

- A *Social Story*™ about the importance of visiting the doctor
- A step-by-step approach numbered one to ten (as detailed in the hairdressing visit) may also help
- A "first and then" board as detailed in the "dental appointment strategies"

Figure 4.55

School visit (*not* the first day of school)

What	Possible reasons why
Displaying anxiety about the school visit	Lack of predictability about the visit: how long will it last, what will happen etc. Auditory hypersensitivity

How you might be able to help

Preparation is key to a successful visit. Plenty of advance notice is required in order to have a smooth transition between home and school. If possible, try to have at least one or two visits to the school before they attend. Below are some top tips which may help:

- Look at the school's website to familiarise your child with the building: looking at layout of classrooms, specific areas, e.g., gym hall, lunch hall, outdoor play areas

- Drive or walk past the school taking the route you will be doing when your child attends. Point out the school as you drive/walk past and smile while doing so – if your child senses tension, this could make them form a negative association with the school

- Plan a visit to the school by yourself (if permitted) and take photographs (if permitted) of all of the areas mentioned above, and also of key people who will be working with your child, e.g., class teacher, classroom assistant(s), lunch hall staff, and janitor. Show these images of the staff and building to your child to familiarise them with these new people and places

- Explain to the staff that on the day your child will be visiting the school, you and your child will only be there for 30 minutes (or however long you think your child could cope with on the day)

Figure 4.56

- About a month before their visit, have a month-to-view calendar to hand and ask your child to cross off each day – circle the day of the visit to show visually how time is passing until the visit. Count the remaining days in terms of sleeps: two more sleeps, one more sleep

- On the day of the visit, set a timer on your phone for how long you expect the visit to last – a 30-minute visit should give enough time for your child to look around and meet some staff. This will give predictability to your child in terms of the time they will be spending there on the day

- While at the school, ask the staff if there is a school timetable that your child will be following; what specific routines are in place, e.g., lining up, following specific routes along corridors, rules around safety, etc.

- Ask for a copy of the school's handbook (if available) and go through this with your child

- After the visit, if your child has coped well, then treat them to a favourite activity, such as a walk in the park or something that you know they will enjoy. Be mindful, however, that this may form part of a routine for your child, so try to keep it to a good routine, e.g., giving them their favourite book or toy when they get home. If, for example, you leave school and immediately go to the toy shop, then this may be an activity that your child may expect each time they leave the school building

Figure 4.56 (Continued)

PART 3 CHILDREN AGED BETWEEN 13 AND 18

The teenage years can be a difficult time for children to navigate, and this is also true for autistic children. This is a time when many changes happen, both physically and emotionally, and these changes can cause real anxiety for many autistic children. Although this part of Chapter 4 is focused on children aged between 13 and 18, it is important to state that puberty can occur for some children between the ages of 8 to 15 (Hattersley 2014), so please bear this in mind.

Some of the aspects of adolescence that autistic teenagers may find challenging are included within this section. It is important to mention again that sections can have a cross over, and so, what may work for one autistic teenager, may not work for another. You will know your child better than anyone, so you can pick and choose those strategies that would be most helpful to your child's particular requirements.

For ease of duplication, the strategies suggested in Part 2 of this chapter could be applied to teenagers too, so Part 3 will focus on specific *teenage* issues and supportive strategies.

Social communication and interaction
(with friends)

What	Possible reasons why
Difficulty with initiating friendships with peers	Autism – social communication and interaction differences
Choosing not to spend time with peers	Fear of saying something inappropriate
	Not finding enjoyment in other people's company
	Not sharing the same interests as their peers

How you might be able to help
This can be a very contentious issue. On the one hand, you have non-autistic well-intentioned people trying to "teach" social skills and encourage autistic teenagers to socialise (because that is what non-autistic people feel is the right course of action). On the other hand, there may be an autistic teenager who may not want to socialise because there is too much anxiety involved in meeting up with other peers. I would listen very carefully to what your teenager wants to do. Luke Jackson (2002) – an autistic teenager at the time of writing his book, speaking to fellow autistic teenagers, says that if they (autistic teenagers) are happy to be on their own, then they shouldn't be pushed into having friendships. It is important also to highlight here that this section is to provide strategies that may help to alleviate some anxiety in social situations, *not* to try to "shoehorn" them into situations in which they may feel discomfort. It may be the case that there are other neurodivergent children with whom they may feel more comfortable, and this should also be encouraged. It's also important to say that non-autistic children would benefit from having a greater awareness of their neurodivergent peers, and strategies that *they* could use when socialising with them.
If your autistic teenager does show a real interest in meeting with others, but doesn't know where to begin, then the following strategies could help:
• Suggest that they join a club either in or out of school, where other peers have similar interests, e.g., chess club, art club, swimming, cycling, etc. They may not be comfortable with the idea of joining a club, so please respect this decision

Figure 4.57

- Teach your child some conversation "starters", e.g., "Hi, my name's . . . I see you like . . . I like that too"

- Practise having these conversations with your teenager in a role play scenario – if they are comfortable to do this

- Explain that the conversation may not go exactly as you have practised, detailing what could happen; the person could end the conversation abruptly, the person may interrupt what your teenager is saying, or someone else may end the conversation by interrupting

- Give practical suggestions about what to do if the conversation ends unexpectedly, such as a phrase to use, e.g., "ok, well, see you later"

- Discuss body language cues – what are the telltale signs that someone is bored with a conversation: if they are always looking away when you are speaking, if they look at their watch, if they begin yawning

- Suggest that if they are talking about their special interest(s), then advise them about an appropriate timeframe for this. For example, if they wish to talk about their favourite television show, then remind them that this might not be what the other person wants to talk about, and to be aware of this

- Encourage them to ask what the other person is interested in, enjoys or simply how they are feeling

- Encourage them to wait until the person has finished speaking before they begin to speak – interrupting someone mid-sentence can appear rude, but your autistic teenager may just be really enthusiastic to participate in the conversation, and not appreciate that this could be viewed as being rude

- If your child feels uncomfortable in the conversation, suggest ways to end the chat, e.g., looking at their watch saying "oh look at the time, I need to go, it was good to see you, speak to you soon" or some other comment that will provide an ending

Figure 4.57 (Continued)

Puberty

What	Possible reasons why
Anxiety	1 Body changing: getting taller, growing facial and pubic hair, voice breaking, growing breasts
	2 Menstruation
	3 Heightened emotions due to hormonal changes
How you might be able to help	

Autistic people need to know the "why" more than their non-autistic peers (Rowe 2015). So it is very important that you explain to your autistic teenager why their body is changing, and, more importantly, how you can help them to understand what they can do to feel less anxious about it. Here are some suggestions on how to do this:

1

- Explain to them that everyone on the planet goes through puberty, it is the body's way of changing from being a child to an adult. It can start at different times for different people, and it is a very natural thing to happen

- Be very factual about describing how the body changes using the correct medical terminology, e.g., penis, vagina. Also explain other names that people may use for these parts of the body, and when it is appropriate to use these other words, and when it is not . . . This is not a time for discussing "the birds and the bees"

- Talk about how your teenager's body will be (or has been) changing; if they are getting taller, if they are starting to have facial hair, if they are developing breasts, if their hips are becoming a little fuller. Explain that all of these things have happened to people that your teenager knows, e.g., you and every adult they know. They may need reassurance that this is a normal pattern of development, so look at medical books with drawings of how the body changes through puberty and discuss these

Figure 4.58

- Show photographs of you as a child, and then as a teenager and throughout your adolescent years. This will give a visual representation of how your body has developed, how you've grown and changed over the years as an example. Explain that these changes do not happen overnight, and that it takes time, just like a seed turning into a flower, it doesn't happen overnight

- If your teenager is a boy, then have his dad or another close male relative explain about how their voice "broke", showing pre- and post-videos if possible. Explain that the voice box (larynx) in boys grows as the body gets older, and so the voice will become deeper, and that this is perfectly natural

2 This can be a very frightening time for young girls, and so it is a good idea to be prepared for their first period, rather than wait until it has happened. So when is a good time to begin this tricky conversation? Typically, young girls will begin menstruation about 2 years from when their breasts begin to grow and about 2 year after first experiencing a white vaginal discharge (see www.nhs.uk). Here are some strategies to help with this preparation:

- Where possible, use only correct medical terminology, but as before, explain the different words people can use for menstruating and the parts of the body

- Use visuals (preferably medical drawings) as a supplement to what you are saying

- Explain why women menstruate and that when the time comes, you will be there to help them

- Show an example of what their underwear may look like when they are menstruating using a red food dye (Rowe 2015). This will give a visual representation of what they can expect to see, and will make it less frightening for them when it happens

- Discuss – using real products – sanitary towels and how to put these on underwear

Figure 4.58 (Continued)

- Explain the frequency and duration of menstruation, and that it can happen every 28 days, but can happen maybe a day or two earlier or later each month

- Talk about when sanitary towels should be changed, and about keeping clean during this time

- Buy a pack of sanitary towels and have these in your child's underwear drawer until needed

When the first menstruation occurs:

- Remain calm, the calmer you are in your responses, the less anxious they may be

- Remind them of the chat about the sanitary towels and guide them to cleaning themselves and discussing how and when to put one on

- Explain that they will need to wear a sanitary towel even at night in bed

- Explain that while menstruating, activities involving being in a swimming pool are not suitable

- Mark off on a large month-to-view calendar with a small red dot when this first period occurred, and use this as a countdown for the next one. This will give predictability to them, and enable them to know roughly when to prepare for the next time

3 Heightened emotions are very common among teenagers, and autistic teenagers are no exception. What can make it extra difficult for autistic teenagers is that can quite often they struggle to understand these emotions, and can as a result, become very anxious, and, in some cases, suicidal. Autistic people are at a greater risk of suicide than non-autistic people (see autism.org. uk). This statistic isn't meant to frighten you, but rather, it is to suggest that you try to be mindful of this information during your child's adolescent years. Here are some strategies that may

Figure 4.58 (Continued)

help your child with these heightened emotions and anxiety through the teenage years:

- Speak regularly to your autistic teenager and ask them how they are feeling. It may be that they don't know how to respond using words, but perhaps using a visual scale may help. For example, a happiness scale could be numbered 1–5 with 1 representing "really happy" to 5 representing "really sad"

- Ask them if they would like to keep an emotions diary: numbering 1–5 with how they are feeling each day. Don't pressurise them into doing this if they are not keen to do so. They could also record how they are feeling at the end of the day using the 1–5 scale by writing the number on a month-to-view calendar. This could also show up any patterns in how they are feeling, e.g., are they always a 5 when it is a Monday or when it is time to go for the weekly shop . . .

- Explain that there is no right or wrong way to feel, and validate any feelings that they share with you

- If they let you know that they are at a number 5 on the scale, ask what could they or you do to make it a 4 or a 3

- Allow your teenager time to participate in their special interest if they have one. This can help to reduce anxiety by allowing them to engage in familiar and enjoyable activities

- Avoid putting pressure on your autistic teenager to participate in activities that they need not do, e.g., activities that will give them anxiety

- Suggest useful apps that monitor how a person is feeling – these can be found on the NHS website or on autism.org.uk. Quite often, teenagers are on their mobile phones, so having an app that is portable and instant can be comforting and reassuring – see Chapter 5 for suitable apps

Figure 4.58 (Continued)

- Try not to project your own worries and fears onto them by discussing them with your teenager. This can add to their own worries and only cause more anxiety for them, so best to talk about any problems or concerns you have with someone else in your family or with your friends. Equally, try not to discuss major problems happening elsewhere in the world, e.g., bad news stories. These can also be concerning for autistic teenagers, and can also give them anxiety

- Focusing on good news stories and happy events can lift anyone's mood, so watching a familiar funny film or comedian on television can really help to alleviate any anxiety and tension too

Figure 4.58 (Continued)

Personal hygiene

What	Possible reasons why
Body odour	1 Not noticing that they need to wash each day, and are possibly unaware of the importance of personal hygiene 2 Sensory sensitivities due to taste, smell, and touch

How you might be able to help

1

- Establish a good personal hygiene routine with your teenager. Use visuals to help with this (if needed)
- Explain why it is important to wash regularly and how their body is changing and that they are producing sweat, which can smell unpleasant to others
- Use a comic strip conversation (see autism.org.uk) to explain how not washing their body can affect them with their peers

2

- Toothpaste and mouthwashes can be very strong, so consider using non-flavoured equivalents
- Suggest an electric toothbrush if they seek oral feedback. Electric toothbrushes are more predictable in their movement than manual ones. If they are avoiding oral feedback, use a soft bristle brush or chewable toothpaste
- Encourage the use of a roll-on deodorant instead of a spray one can help to minimise the smell when applying
- Provide unscented soap and a soft natural sponge
- Suggest shampoo and conditioner in one bottle for convenience

Figure 4.59

- Use a bath mat for security to prevent accidental slipping
- Try using swimming goggles in the shower if soap or shampoo getting in their eyes gives them anxiety
- Have a hot towel ready when coming out of the bath or shower. This will ease the transition between coming out of the heat into the cold
- Finger and toe nail clipping can be traumatic for autistic children. Doing this after a bath or shower will be easier for them as the nails will be softer. Always encourage them to snip a tiny bit at a time to avoid taking too much off

Figure 4.59 (Continued)

Vulnerabilities

What	Possible reasons why
1 Inappropriate touch from others 2 Being bullied at school 3 Being bullied on social media	1 Not having an awareness or understanding that certain parts of the body are private 2 There are no acceptable reasons for bullying another person. Autistic children, however, are more vulnerable to being bullied (Hattersley 2014) 3 As above
How you might be able to help	

1 This is where many young autistic adolescents are vulnerable. Unfortunately, there are many people who are only too willing to take advantage of young boys and girls, and when you factor in the differences in social communication and interaction, it can be quite an anxious time for both the teenager and their parents. Here are some strategies that may help your autistic teenager:

- Talk your autistic teenager about "private parts" of the body. Again, please use the proper terminology: penis, testicles, bottom, vagina, inner thighs, breasts, bottom (Hattersley 2014). Use medical drawings to show as examples

- Discuss who is allowed to touch these areas of their body, e.g., a doctor or nurse might ask them to undress and touch these areas if examining them

- Talk about what it means to be naked and where it is ok to be naked, e.g., in their own bedroom with the door shut, or in the bathroom with the door shut and locked, but not if someone asks them on their phone or online

- Discuss what topics of conversation are private, e.g., their private parts, masturbating, menstruation, going to the toilet, shaving, personal hygiene, sexual thoughts about boys/girls. Again, stress that it is not ok for someone online to ask them personal questions about their body or have these types of discussion

Figure 4.60

2 Bullying can be a common experience for autistic teenagers, and it can be very frightening for them to understand why people can be so cruel to others. Sometimes their friends can bully them without their knowing, so it is important to give them some strategies to help to cope, should they experience it. Here are some ways that may help them:

- If you suspect that your autistic teenager is being bullied, then it is important to explain what it means to be bullied, and explaining some of the actions that a bully might do to them including name calling, hitting, saying unkind words or deliberately ignoring them, making fun of them by mimicking them, or taking advantage of them by taking money from them

- If your child is not able to discuss what is happening to them face to face, then it might help if they can email or write you a note about what is happening with a who/what/where/when format. This might make it easier for them to communicate any issues to you

- It may also help them to draw pictures of what happened and what was said

- If they don't feel comfortable discussing their concerns with you at all, then signpost them to people who may be able to help them; someone else in the family, a trusted teacher at school, or the "Childline" helpline

- If they do feel comfortable discussing events that have happened, then try to not to become angry or agitated. It will obviously be very upsetting for you to hear what is, or has been happening to them, but remaining calm may help them to feel less stressed, and more comfortable in sharing their experiences with you

- Agree a plan with them on how it can best be tackled. Please don't promise them that you will stop the bullying, unless you are with them 24 hours of the day, then there is a chance that the bully may still be around, and your teenager may lose trust in what you say should the bullying continue

- Ask them to keep a record of any bullying that they experience including dates and times, and if anyone else were there to witness it. This is good evidence to take to their teacher or the person in charge of their year group

Figure 4.60 (Continued)

- Be honest with them, if you want to speak to their teacher or the person in charge of their year group, then explain to them why it is important that this should happen; they may be able to help stop the bully, or they may be able to make other arrangements so that the bully cannot get access to them

- See References for more information on bullying at school

3 Social media nowadays can reach young people at any time of the day or night, and in any location. As many young teenagers have almost constant access to their mobile phones or gaming devices, it is important to teach them about keeping safe online. The following may help with this:

- If you are concerned that your child is showing signs of being cyberbullied, then it is important to have a conversation about this with them and discuss different people who can help them (see www.nspcc.org.uk). This may be a trusted teacher, a friend or a relative

- www.thinkyouknow.co.uk also provides specific advice for different age groups, and gives practical suggestions on how to report cyber bullying and whom to contact should they have any concerns

- https://cerebra.org.uk/download/learning-disabilities-autism-and-internet-safety/ discusses how to keep autistic children safe online, and has a helpful section for parents

Figure 4.60 (Continued)

Hopefully, this chapter of the book has given you some useful strategies for supporting your autistic child in a variety of areas as they grow and develop. Let's now look at what further support is available.

CHAPTER 5

Further support

A lot of misinformation exists about autism, so this chapter will hopefully guide you to access further help and support you and your family may seek to support your autistic child.

The list of resources detailed within the chapter is not exhaustive; there are so many good sources of information that it would not be possible to list all of them in this book.

I have found these resources to be very informative and useful, but please feel free to do your own research on what is particularly relevant for your own child's individual circumstances. The information in this chapter is listed as follows:

- Information about autism: books and internet sites
- Organisations and support programmes for parents
- Games, toys, sensory resources, and apps
- Financial support
- Support for education
- Other support

Please be guided also by the autistic community; autistic adults have first-hand knowledge about autism, and this is so invaluable. Within the next section, there is a list containing books written by autistic authors. So let's look now at some of these resources, beginning with books.

BOOKS

Books about autism written by autistic authors
Freaks, Geeks and Asperger Syndrome, by Luke Jackson.
Odd Girl Out: An Autistic Woman in a Neurotypical World, by Laura James.

DOI: 10.4324/9781003122227-5

Funny, You Don't Look Autistic, by Michael McCreary.
Divergent Mind: Thriving in a World That Wasn't Designed for You, by Jenara Nerenberg.

Books about autism
[Full details available in the References.]

Autism & Asperger Syndrome in Children, by Luke Beardon.
Uniquely Human, by Barry M. Prizant, with Tom Fields-Meyer.
Neurotribes: The Legacy of Autism and How to Think Smarter About People Who Think Differently, by S. Silberman.
Girls and Autism, by Barry Carpenter, Francesca Happe, and Jo Egerton.

Books about communication
The New Social Story™ Book, by Carole Gray.
More Than Words, by Fern Sussman.

Books to support siblings of autistic children
Leah's Voice, by Lori Demonia.
A Sibling's Guide to Autism, by Irene Kim.

Books to support toileting
The Potty Journey, by Judith A. Coucouvanis.
Where Does My Poo Go?, by Jo Lindley.

Internet sites
There are many sites about autism on the internet. These ones listed here offer good advice and sources of information:

https://swanscotland.org
https://www.autism.org.uk
https://www.nhs.uk/conditions/autism/
https://www.scottishautism.org
https://www.thirdspace.scot/nait/

These websites are particularly useful if sensory resources are required:

https://sensetoys.com
https://www.cheapdisabilityaids.co.uk

If you are looking for sensory strategies, then the following websites could help:

https://www.autism.org.uk/advice-and-guidance/topics/sensory-differences/sensory-differences/all-audiences
https://www.falkirk.gov.uk/services/social-care/disabilities/docs/young-people/Making%20Sense%20of%20Sensory%20Behaviour.pdf?v=201906271131

If you are seeking good visual schedules, then the following websites are useful:

https://do2learn.com
https://goboardmaker.com/pages/boardmaker-7
https://www.widgit.com/about-symbols/index.htm

For information about communication, these websites are helpful:

http://www.hanen.org/Home.aspx
https://ican.org.uk
https://www.autism.org.uk/advice-and-guidance/topics/communication

For information about sleeping:

https://sleepscotland.org
https://thesleepcharity.org.uk

SUPPORT PROGRAMMES FOR PARENTS AND CARERS

The National Autistic Society runs the following programmes for parents and carers:

"EarlyBird" – for children under the age of 5
"EarlyBird Plus" – for children aged between 4 and 9
"Teen Life" – for teenage children

For more information: https://www.autism.org.uk/what-we-do/support-in-the-community/family-support

Barnardo's run the "Cygnet" programme for children between the ages of 5 and 18:

https://barnardos-parenting.org.uk/cygnet-programme/

Hanen – "More Than Words" – for children up to age 5 and "Talkability" – for able children aged between 4 and 8:

http://www.hanen.org/Programs/For-Parents/More-Than-Words.aspx

Scottish Autism – "Right click" for parents and carers:

https://www.scottishautism.org/services-support/family-support/online-support-rightclick

There are many more online courses, but quite a few of these will charge a fee to participate.

GAMES, TOYS, SENSORY RESOURCES, AND APPS

Please note that your autistic child may not initially be interested in toys. It can be helpful therefore to try to elicit how they *do* enjoy spending their time. For example, if they enjoy watching clothes spinning around in the washing machine, then games or toys that have this effect may give them the same pleasure. If their enjoyment is flicking switches on and off, then a purpose-built toy that has this same element within it might be a better idea. If you know a handy carpenter, then a purpose-built board containing switches that are not connected to an electricity supply would be a good alternative. Similarly, if your child enjoys opening and closing doors, then there are some toys available with miniature doors and locks that would give them the same pleasure, but without disturbing others in the house.

It is important to stress that if your child simply enjoys lining up cars rather than playing with them in a traditional manner, then as long as they are gaining enjoyment from this, who has the right to stop this form of play? Similarly, if your child seeks play through sensory means, then this should not be discouraged.

The following is a list of games and toys that I have successfully used with autistic children over the years – please note that it is important that these are just suggestions, and, for safety purposes, please check whether the age range of any product detailed is suitable for your child before you purchase it.

There is not an age range mentioned for these games or activities, as they may be used at different ages dependent on your child's needs, ability, or preferences.

Also included is a list of sensory activities and toys that can be used, should your child prefer to participate in this form of play.

"Cause and effect" games
- Wind-up toys
- Higolot™ Toddler Busy Cube Montessori Educational Toy
- Fun time Pop Up Farmyard Friends
- Bright Starts Press and Glow Spinner
- Car ramp racer
- Jack-in–the–Box
- Melissa & Doug™ Lock and Latch Board
- Casdon™ Electronic Washer
- Shape sorter

Sensory toys/activities
Visual
- Spinning top
- Lava lamp (battery operated)

- Bubble wand
- Light up/spinning wand

Auditory
- Noise makers such as a "Groan" tube or a Rainmaker
- Piano floor mat
- Echo microphone
- Melissa & Doug™ Sound Puzzle

Tactile
- Theraputty™
- Koosh Ball
- Bubblewrap for popping (with supervision)
- "Gloop" – Mixing cornflour with water – two parts cornflour to one part water (check for allergies beforehand) – you can also add food colouring to make it more enticing (allergies permitting)

Olfactory
- Scented play dough
- Scented bubbles
- Scratch and sniff books
- Scented fidget toys

Gustatory
- Helping to prepare simple snacks
- Finger foods
- Baking cakes and biscuits
- Taste testing different foods

Vestibular
- Swings
- Roundabouts
- Seesaws
- Trampolines

Proprioception
- Hand-held massager
- Vibrating cuddly toys
- Ball pool
- Tactile "bumpy" balls

Interoception
- Dress Teddy for a cold day/warm day – teaching about hot/cold
- Emotions finger puppets – teaching about internal emotions
- Greedy Gorilla game (Orchard Toys) – teaching about healthy foods and feeling full
- "Simon says" – can be used to regulate emotions, e.g., "Simon says: Take a deep breath, jump on the spot, now feel your heart beat." This game can be used to make a young child aware of what their body is telling them; they are hot, cold, heart is beating quickly or slowly, if they are calm, etc.

Apps

There are lots of apps that can offer support for a variety of different purposes. Please use your discretion when deciding if these, or any apps, are suitable for your child or teenager. Some examples of apps are listed as follows.

For communication
Call Scotland (https://www.callscotland.org.uk) has produced an app "wheel" specifically for augmentative and alternative communication:

> https://www.callscotland.org.uk/common-assets/cm-files/posters/ipad-apps-for-complex-communication-support-needs.pdf

When entering this link, there is a downloadable version of the communication "wheel" where apps can be accessed directly, giving you an insight into each of them.

For visual schedules
"Choiceworks" app: only available on Apple devices and there is a charge
"Kids ToDo List" app: available on Apple and Android devices

For time tracking
"TimeTrack – Visual timer": available on Apple devices
"Kids Timer": available on Apple and Android devices

For sensory/relaxation
"Pop it Master – calm": available on Apple and Android devices
"Just touch too": available on Apple and Android devices

FINANCIAL SUPPORT

In the United Kingdom, autism is classed as a disability, and, as such, financial support is available for your autistic child

In Scotland, you can apply for "child disability payment" (https://www.mygov.scot/ child-disability-payment)

In England and Wales, you can apply for "disability living allowance" (https://www.gov.uk/disability-living-allowance-children)

In Northern Ireland, you can apply for "disability living allowance". (https://www.nidirect.gov.uk/articles/disability-living-allowance-children)

Please note that there are specific eligibility criteria on each of the websites mentioned, and different allowances may apply depending on the age of the child

The National Autistic Society has a comprehensive list of sources of support on this link: https://www.autism.org.uk/advice-and-guidance/topics/benefits-and-money/benefits/benefits-you-can-get/benefits-for-autistic-children

The Family Fund is a UK charity that provides grants to families of disabled children, and their website can be accessed via this link: https://www.familyfund.org.uk

SUPPORT FOR EDUCATION

https://www.autism.org.uk/advice-and-guidance/topics/ education/extra-help-at-school/scotland
https://www.autism.org.uk/advice-and-guidance/topics/ education/extra-help-at-school/england
https://www.autism.org.uk/advice-and-guidance/topics/ education/extra-help-at-school/northern-ireland
https://www.autism.org.uk/advice-and-guidance/topics/ education/extra-help-at-school/wales

OTHER SUPPORT

Your local authority may also have a "One Stop Shop" for autism – a place where you can access more local help for you and/or your autistic child. Ask at your local council headquarters for more information, or search online to see if there is one near you. There may also be local autism groups in your area. A quick internet search may yield this information. These local groups are especially helpful for people to meet and share experiences, ideas, and strategies of support. They are also great places for simply having a cup of tea and a chat with people who may share similar experiences.

CHAPTER 6

Looking to the future with positivity

It is important to say that while your autistic child has reached the age of adulthood at 18, they may still require support in the future. This chapter will look at what you can do to support your autistic child with the transition into adulthood.

But first, let's look at some key messages that you can take from this book:

- Be calm – never underestimate the effect that your responses have on your child
- Be consistent – this is such an important message
- Give predictability to events – sudden surprises can cause problems for some autistic people
- Please don't insist on eye contact
- Please be very mindful of sensory sensitivities
- Explain new events or people visually, and give advance notice of any new changes
- Reduce your level of language to meet your child's level of understanding – too much may overload and confuse
- Use visuals (where required) to explain routines or planned events – this will give predictability and a sense of security to your child

These are just some of the key messages that can help you to help your child. Like most parents, however, you will be thinking about their future, and will want to ensure that when they reach adulthood, they will have a job, a relationship, and a place of their own to call home.

As mentioned previously in this book, no two autistic individuals are the same, and so what may work for one autistic young adult may not be appropriate for another.

DOI: 10.4324/9781003122227-6

The most important advice I can give you is to be positive about their future. Try not to limit their potential, but, instead, aim high. Too often, young autistic adults are denied opportunities to flourish because their differences are not understood by others. Try to teach your child that they are worth more than the opinions of those who do not understand these differences.

When thinking about work options, incorporating their special interests or talents can be very helpful. For example, if the special interest is trains, then perhaps applying for a job working on a train or in a railway station might be of interest. Similarly, if the special interest is in autism, then working with autistic adults or teaching might be a good career choice. There are many professions in which autistic people do remarkably well due to their level of interest, knowledge of the subject, and attention to detail. One of these is the medical profession. There are many autistic doctors, surgeons, and professors who are experts in their field.

There are also many autistic people who work within the technology and information technology sectors. Many autistic youngsters are quite skilful in using a computer, and in one job I did many years ago, we would heavily rely on one of our autistic young adults to help us out with any IT problems when our technology expert was stumped about how to solve the problem.

Try to encourage your high school autistic teenager to think about the skill sets they have, rather than spending time thinking about those areas where they may need support. Very often young autistic people will not like to fail, and see failure in a particular subject area as a weakness. It's important to shift that focus on to the positive elements of their school work, with a view to looking at how these positive skills can help them to find a career that they would enjoy.

Employers in the United Kingdom have a legal obligation to interview disabled applicants for jobs, and to make reasonable adjustments to accommodate disabilities within the workplace (see www.gov.uk) – autism, as mentioned earlier in the book, is classed in the UK as a disability.

There are many young autistic people who will help fellow "autists" navigate their way through career choices and be there to offer support via platforms such as Twitter™ and other social media.

Whatever choices your autistic child makes in life, one thing is for certain: with you as their knowledgeable advocate and supporter, they can only flourish and thrive.

I wish you and your child, or grandchild, well, on your journey of discovery together.

Glossary

ADHD – attention deficit hyperactivity disorder – a condition whose main characteristics are inattention, hyperactivity, and impulsive actions.

ASC – autism spectrum condition (autism). This term is used to describe autism and avoids the use of the word "disorder", which carries connotations of a "deficit model" of autism; something that is widely unpopular with autistic people.

ASD – autism spectrum disorder (autism). This term was first used in the *DSM-5* in 2013 and was used to combine other forms of autism under one "spectrum". The use of the word "disorder" is widely disliked within the autism community, but is used as the medical terminology to describe autism (see autism.org.uk).

ASP – additional support plan – an individual educational plan that identifies a pupil's strengths and development needs. It addresses how the educational establishment aims to support these needs.

Asperger syndrome – named after Hans Asperger (working in the 1940s) – this diagnosis within the autism spectrum is no longer given for newly diagnosed autistic people.

Aspie – someone who has a diagnosis of Asperger syndrome.

Autie or autist – someone who is autistic.

Central coherence – a way of thinking that allows a person to see the "big picture". Someone with strong central coherence is able to transfer skills, categorise information, and obtain a main idea from a conversation or piece of writing.

CSP – Co-ordinated support plan – a statutory document compiled for children and young people with enduring and complex additional support needs. A high level of co-ordination from education and other agencies outwith education is required.

Delayed echolalia – repetition of words and/or phrases days or even weeks after hearing.

Diagnostic and Statistical Manual (DSM-5) – a system used for diagnosing autism, published by the American Psychiatric Association (APA).

Echolalia – repetition of previously heard words and/or phrases.

Emotional regulation – the way in which a person manages how they feel in response to external events and circumstances, and in how they perceive and act on these feelings.

Executive function – a term referring to how a person plans, organises, and controls their impulses, manages their time, understands difficult concepts, and uses new approaches. It also relates to their working memory.

ICD 10 and *ICD 11* – *International Classification of Diseases* – 10th and 11th editions, published by the World Health Organisation. This is a commonly used method of diagnosing autism in the UK (*ICD 11* replaced *ICD 10* in 2022).

Intensive interaction – a practical way of interacting with people with learning disabilities who require support with communicating.

Joint attention – when a common focus on an object, person, concept, or event is shared with another person.

Neurodivergent – a term used to describe differences in neurological development or function to typical (predominant) neurological development or function.

Neurodiversity – a term used to describe the idea that neurological differences such as autism and ADHD are variations in the human genome, rather than conditions that have been historically pathologised by doctors.

Neurotypical (NT) – a term used to describe the predominant non-autistic individual.

Stimming – self-stimulating actions that are evident when an autistic person is stressed or excited. These can vary in type and can include the flapping of hands, jumping, flicking fingers together, hand "wringing", or making noises.

Theory of mind – a term referring to a person being able to put themselves in another's shoes: to recognise and appreciate other people's feelings, thoughts, and intentions. The "Sally-Anne" test is a visual example of this in action (available if you type "sally-anne test" into an internet search engine.

References

American Psychiatric Association (APA) (2013). *Diagnostic and Statistical Manual of Mental Disorders*, 5th edn. Washington, DC: American Psychiatric Association.

Autism Toolbox *Communication*. Available from http://www.autismtoolbox.co.uk/ communication. Retrieved on 9 July 2020.

Beardon, L. (2019). *Autism & Asperger Syndrome in Children*. London: Sheldon Press.

Carpenter, B., Happe, F., and Egerton, J. (2019). *Girls and Autism*. Abingdon: Routledge.

Cerebra.org.uk. *Learning Disabilities, Autism and Internet Safety*. Available from https://cerebra.org.uk/download/learning-disabilities-autism-and-internet-safety/. Retrieved on 30 August 2020.

Childline.org.uk. *Bullying, Abuse, Safety & The Law*. Available from https://www.childline.org.uk/info-advice/bullying-abuse-safety/. Retrieved on 2 March 2022.

Civardi, A. (2020). *Going to the Doctor*. London: Usborne Publishing Ltd.

Civardi, A. (2021). *Going to the Dentist*. London: Usborne Publishing Ltd.

Corscadden, P. and Casserly, A. (2021). Identification of Autism in Girls: Role of Trait Subtleties, Social Acceptance and Masking, *REACH: Journal of Inclusive Education in Ireland*, 34.1. 18–28.

Coucouvanis, J.A. (2008). *The Potty Journey*. Kansas: AAPC Publishing.

Dean, M., Harwood, R., and Kasari, C. (2017). The Art of Camouflage: Gender Differences in the Social Behaviors of Girls and Boys with Autism Spectrum Disorder, *Autism*, 21. 678–689.

Gordon, I., Pierce, Bartlett, M.S., and Tanaka, J.W. (2014). Training Facial Expression Production in Children on the Autism Spectrum, *Journal of Autism Development Disorder*, 44. 2486–2498.

Grandin, T. (2020). *Different Not Less*, 2nd edn. Arlington: Future Horizons Publishing.

Grandin, T. and Barron, S. (2017). *Unwritten Rules of Social Relationships: Decoding Social Mysteries Through the Unique Perspectives of Autism*. Arlington: Future Horizons Publishing.

Gray, C. (2015). *The New Social Story™ Book*. Arlington: Future Horizons Publishing.

Hattersley, C. (2014). *Autism: Supporting Your Teenager*. London: National Autistic Society.

ican.org.uk. *Parents – Ages and Stages*. Available from https://ican.org.uk/i-cans-talking-point/parents/ages-and-stages/. Retrieved on 17 July 2020.

Jackson, L. (2002). *Freaks, Geeks and Asperger Syndrome*. London: Jessica Kingsley Publishers.

James, L. (2018). *Odd Girl Out: An Autistic Woman in a Neurotypical World*. London: Pan Macmillan.

Jones, E.A. Carr, E.G. (2004). Joint Attention in Children with Autism; Theory and Intervention, *Focus on Autism and Other Developmental Disabilities*, 19. 13–26.

Kim, I. (2021). *A Sibling's Guide to Autism*. Published by Irene Kim.

Leniston, T. Grounds, R. (2018). *Coming Home to Autism A Room-by-Room Approach to Supporting Your Child at Home after ASD Diagnosis*. London: Jessica Kingsley Publishers.

Lindley, J. (2021). *Where Does My Poo Go?* London: DK Children.

Lowry, L. (2016). *3 Things You Should Know About Echolalia*. Available from http://www.hanen.org/Helpful-Info/Articles/3-Things-You-Should-Know-About-Echolalia.aspx. Retrieved on 12 December 2020.

Makaton.org. https://makaton.org

McCreary (2019). *Funny, You Don't Look Autistic: A Comedian's Guide to Life on the Spectrum*. Toronto: Annick Press.

National Autistic Society. *Autistic Women and Girls*. Available from https://www.autism.org.uk/advice-and-guidance/what-is-autism/autistic-women-and-girls. Retrieved on 1 July 2020.

National Autistic Society. *Dealing with Bullying*. Available from https://www.autism.org.uk/advice-and-guidance/topics/bullying/bullying. Retrieved on 23 August 2020.

National Autistic Society. *Eating – A Guide For All Audiences*. Available from https://www.autism.org.uk/advice-and-guidance/topics/behaviour/eating/all-audiences. Retrieved on 1 July 2020.

National Autistic Society: *Sensory Differences A Guide For All Audiences*. Available from https://www.autism.org.uk/advice-and-guidance/topics/sensory-differences/sensory-differences/all-audiences. Retrieved on 23 August 2020.

National Autistic Society. *Sleep and Autism*. Available from https://www.autism.org.uk/advice-and-guidance/topics/physical-health/sleep. Retrieved on 21 December 2020.

National Autistic Society. *Social Stories and Comic Strip Conversations*. Available from https://www.autism.org.uk/advice-and-guidance/topics/communication/communication-tools/social-stories-and-comic-strip-conversations. Retrieved on 1 July 2020.

National Autistic Society. *What is Anxiety?* Available from https://www.autism.org.uk/advice-and-guidance/topics/mental-health/anxiety#Why%20might%20autistic%20people%20experience%20anxiety? Retrieved on 8 July 2020.

Nerenberg, J. (2020). *Divergent Mind: Thriving in a World That Wasn't Designed for You*. San Francisco: HarperOne.

NHS. *Food Colours and Hyperactivity*. Available from https://www.nhs.uk/con ditions/food-colours-and-hyperactivity/. Retrieved 8 July 2020.

NHS. *What Is Autism?* Available from https://www.nhs.uk/conditions/autism/what-is-autism/. Retrieved on 1 July 2020.

Patten, E., Belardi, K., Baranek, G.T., Watson, L.R., Labban, J.D., and Oller, D.K. (2014). Vocal Patterns in Infants with Autism Spectrum Disorder: Canonical Babbling Status and Vocalization Frequency, *Journal of Autism Development Disorder*,44(10). 2413–2428

Prizant, B.M., with T. Fields-Meyer (2015). *Uniquely Human – A Different Way of Seeing Autism*. London: Souvenir Press.

Pyramid Educational Consultants. *PECS*. Available from https://pecs-unitedk ingdom.com. Retrieved on 20 February 2022.

Rowe, A. (2015). *Asperger's Syndrome and Puberty*. London: Lonely Mind Books.

Silberman, S. (2015). *Neurotribes: The Legacy of Autism and How to Think Smarter About People Who Think Differently*. London: Allen & Unwin.

Smith, M.A., Segal, J., and Hutman, T. (2020). *Does My Child Have Autism?* Available from https://www.helpguide.org/articles/autism-learning-disa bilities/does-my-child-have-autism.htm. Retrieved on 5 December 2020.

Sussman, F. (2012). *More Than Words: A Parent's Guide to Building Interaction and Language Skills for Children with Autism Spectrum Disorder or Social Communication Difficulties*, 2nd edn. Toronto: Hanen Centre.

Thinkuknow.co.uk. *Cyber Security: A Guide for Parents and Carers*. Available from https://www.thinkuknow.co.uk/parents/articles/parents-guide-to-cyber-security/. Retrieved on 30 August 2020.

Van der Horst, F.C.P., Van Rosmalen, L., and Van der Veer, R. (2020). The Nature of Love: Harlow, Bowlby and Bettelheim on Affectionless Mothers, *History of Psychiatry*, 31(2). 227–231.

Index

Note: References in **bold** are to the Glossary, those in *italics* are to figures.

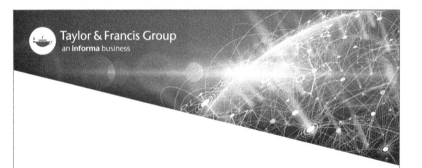

Lightning Source UK Ltd.
Milton Keynes UK
UKHW020007140922
408832UK00006B/74